THANK
you DO!
Jerry & Lorry

God's
One Liners

GOD'S ONE LINERS
© 2011 by Jerry and Jody Tyson

Printed in the United States of America

ISBN 1-933641-42-8

God's One Liners

Devotional Thoughts on the
Shortest Verses in the Bible

Jerry and Jody Tyson

Introduction

A "One Liner" is usually thought of as a brief, funny comment by a comedian. Since the Bible is not a book of humor, we will need to find a different and more fitting description for what follows on these pages.

Our normal impression is, "If it is small, it is of little value." That is true of a penny; true if all a hungry person receives is a few crumbs; and surely true of a two-bedroom house for a family of nine.

It is NOT true of a small verse of scripture. Most folks have a built-in bias against "little" things, but remember, it was a little maid who was the key to Naaman being healed of leprosy. It was the little bit of meal and oil in the widow's pantry that God miraculously used to save her, her son, and the prophet Elijah from starvation. It was a couple of mites, the smallest coins of the day, that Jesus considered to be a large offering because it was all the giver had. It was a young boy's little lunch that fed thousands of hungry people after it was blessed by the Lord.

The lyrics of an old song say, "Little is much when God is in it." One who has walked with God knows this is true. We think you will have to agree by the end of this effort that even the shortest of Bible verses can be long on message.

We will be examining the shortest verses in the order they appear in the New Testament, as well as some selected from the Old Testament. We hope you will find them useful as devotional reading. Perhaps you will find something worth sharing with someone else in a Bible study or conversation.

In the course of preparing the manuscript, we were quite surprised at the broad sweep of subject matter involved in these brief verses. We found doctrine, history, teaching, preaching, and prophecy. We found something practical that dealt with nearly every area of our lives and our relationships with the human family here on earth as well as our future home in Heaven.

In 2 Timothy 4:2–4 we find these familiar words: "Preach the word; be instant in season, out of season; reprove, rebuke, exhort with all longsuffering and doctrine. For the time will come when they will not endure sound doctrine; but after their own lusts shall they heap to themselves teachers, having itching ears; And they shall turn away their ears from the truth, and shall be turned unto fables."

Sometimes God used a chapter or even a whole book to deal with spiritual issues. In these pages we will see that sometimes very few words were needed to communicate great truths.

In your own personal Bible, you may find several other verses that take only one line, or you may not find some of these since various printed versions have different type sizes and page layouts. I used a study version of the King James Bible to choose verses that fit on a single printed line because, as a comedian once said, "Even Mason and Dixon had to draw the line somewhere." (Sorry, I had to say it!)

Jerry Tyson
April 5, 2011

Part I

New Testamenmt
One Liners

Matthew 7:1

Judge not, that ye be not judged

This is the first of "God's One Liners" we encounter in the New Testament as we turn the pages of God's Word.

It is part of man's make up to be judgmental. We love to point our fingers at others, wag them, and draw attention to what we may perceive as a shortcoming in another person. What this verse is not forbidding is judging others against a proper standard, but condemning another person for a deed of which we may be just as guilty as they.

There are laws in nature, such as the law of gravity. If you drop an expensive crystal goblet onto a hard surface, it will most certainly break since gravity always draws things downward. The laws of government are designed for our protection and to keep social order. Fortunately for those of us who live in a city, there are zoning laws prohibiting your neighbor from starting a pig farm in his back yard. The laws of God are the foundation of all civil law, first codified in Exodus 20 with the Ten Commandments.

Holding human behavior up to the standard of a proper legal system is a good thing, or else we would not be able to condemn murder, theft, or the reckless driving of one traveling at sixty miles per hour through a school zone full of small children. We often forget that a good legal system and surely God's judgment are based on a fair and righteous standard. In recent years, however, that biblical legal standard is being eroded by those who would prefer Islamic law or other codes that ignore the Bible. The future for America, once considered a "Christian" nation, is getting darker daily as news reports are beginning to be more numerous as they describe legal decisions that go far afield of common sense, let alone God's Word.

This verse is in the middle of the Sermon on the Mount, where Christ offers some of the most practical teaching ever given on a wide variety of subjects that affect our lives every day. This verse is followed with warning for one who would judge someone else by a standard he does not apply to himself: "For with what judgment ye judge, ye shall be judged: and with what measure ye mete, it shall be measured to you again" (Matthew 7:2). Hypocrisy is one of the first things someone will see when looking at another whose motto is, "Do what I say, but don't do what I do."

In John 7:24, the Lord Jesus instructs us to "Judge not according to the appearance, but judge righteous judgment." We surely need to judge others, but we need to do so by the same standard we would apply to ourselves, and we hope that will be the same one God would use.

All these are the beginning of sorrows

Here is an old illustration of how taking verses out of context gets unacceptable results:

Suppose you and I were to start a new religion. Since scripture is not always easy to understand, (especially for someone who is unsaved, as 1 Corinthians 2:14 says: "But the natural man receiveth not the things of the Spirit of God: for they are foolishness unto him: neither can he know them, because they are spiritually discerned") and since many think the Bible is a big and heavy book to lug around, we will use only three verses as our total focus in our new religion. Those three verses are: 1) Matthew 27:5—"And he [Judas] cast down the pieces of silver in the temple, and departed, and went and hanged himself." 2) The words of Jesus in Luke 10:37—"Go, and do thou likewise." And 3) John 13:27—"Then said Jesus unto him, That thou doest, do quickly." Now, friend, here is my question: With these verses forming our total doctrine and teaching, would you like to join our new church?

Needless to say, if such a church existed, it would have a hard time recruiting new members and an even harder time increasing the roll, as its requirements, while few, are a bit extreme. Most people would be unenthusiastic about hanging themselves, let alone doing it any time soon.

There are those who say living the Christian life is hard. They are wrong. It is not hard. It is impossible, if one tries to do it alone. Christ in us is the hope of glory, as Colossians 1:27 says.

Life has its sorrows. Tomorrow has no guarantees, but one thing is sure: someday in the future, when the wars we have seen in our lifetime, when the Middle East turmoil that is daily in the news, the disease, and national disasters, and the endless list of false teachers setting dates or promising prosperity and riches to any and all who follow them seem to have reached their peak, look out! We ain't seen nothin' yet!

We are now seeing just the tip of the iceberg as the sorrows of life will compound as Satan tries to take more and more control in the world. Talk of a megalomaniac! Here was the top angel in Heaven. We think some of the world's leaders today are narcissistic; Satan wrote the book! One look in the mirror and he fell in love with himself. When God judged his sin and threw him and his followers out of Heaven, he hatched a plan to get even. If he couldn't be God, he would separate those God loves from Him forever by causing man to sin. After Christ paid for that sin on the cross, Satan started to work in a believer's mind to keep his thoughts from God and to continue in sin, with the hoped-for result being a fruitless life.

The words of the Lord here refer to the buildup of apostasy and sin that will culminate during the seven-year period yet future, called the Tribulation. We see increasing lawlessness all around us now, but ahead lies that period of time in which the world will come to the edge of complete destruction.

Matthew 24:21–22 is sobering: "For then shall be great tribulation, such as was not since the beginning of the world to this time, no, nor ever shall be. And except those days should be shortened, there should no flesh be saved: but for the elect's sake those days shall be shortened."

At this early juncture in our journey through the "One Liners" of the Word, a good question would be: Are you going to be here to experience that awful time, or have you put your personal faith and trust in Jesus Christ as your Savior from your sins? Romans 3:23 is the legal indictment against all of humanity: "For all have sinned, and come short of the glory of God." God's righteous standard compared to our lives is like "Mutt and Jeff." We are short, God is extremely tall, and there is no way for us to come up to His standard. That's why God stepped into human and history and human flesh to solve our greatest problem. Even though our "wages" for our sins should be death, the gift of God is eternal life through Jesus Christ our Lord (Romans 6:23).

If you have never done so, now is the time you need to personally accept the substitution of Christ's righteousness for your sin by thanking Him for dying in your place and paying the penalty for your sins—now, not later, since no man alive has any guarantee of any more than the breath in his lungs at any given moment. Second Corinthians 6:2 clearly states: ". . . behold, now is the accepted time; behold, now is the day of salvation."

In 2011, a noted radio personality dared to do what Scripture clearly forbids: he set a date for the end of the world, for Judgment Day. His calculations were difficult to understand, and not to the surprise of anyone with a clear knowledge of God's Word, the date he set came and went. Instead of recognizing his error, he claimed the date that had just passed actually was a time of judgment. Then he set a new date. Untold numbers of people continued to follow his false teaching. Many, no doubt, turned away from God and the Bible in disillusionment, having trusted a man, not the Bible. That teacher suffered a stroke soon after the date came and went. God is not mocked!

When the "beginning of sorrows" of this verse actually occurs, those who have trusted in Jesus Christ as their Savior will have already been evacuated from earth. That is part of the reason the Rapture of the church is referred to as "the Blessed Hope." If you have never accepted the free gift of salvation offered by Christ, there is no better time than now. For many people, tomorrow will not come. You can find their names in the obituaries. "Behold, now is the day of salvation."

Matthew 24:25

Behold, I have told you before

Everyone wants to know the future. A number of years ago, a news story reported a convention of fortune tellers in the Midwest that ran afoul of the law for some reason. One of the arresting officers was quick to tell the reporter covering the event, "If they could tell the future, how come they didn't know we would be there to arrest them?" Good question. The future is of great concern to all of us for the same reason: We don't know what it holds.

This verse is in the same passage and context as the previous one. Christ is telling His hearers of the future so they will not fall into its pitfalls. The "last days" of life on earth as we currently know it will be filled with danger.

Most likely, there is not a single person on this planet who has not heard parents or teachers say, "I told you that would happen. Maybe the next time you will listen!" We don't like to be told, "I told you so." It goes against our human nature to be reminded that we did not follow good advice.

In the case of this "One Liner," the Lord Jesus is instructing the Jews of His day of the signs for which to look in advance of His return to earth. During a yet future time, a world dictator, commonly called "the Antichrist," will be in control, causing worldwide death, mayhem, and destruction to such a degree that Jesus warned that no one would remain alive if He didn't bring an early end to that time period (Matthew 24:21–22).

Over the years we have seen different wannabe messiahs, gurus, or other religious leaders come and go after making claims of being the long-awaited one. Some of them have been and will be quite convincing to the point they have been and will be able to deceive true believers. Who can forget Jim Jones leading hundreds to South America, then giving them Kool-Aid laced with poison to drink. The specific point of this passage is that not one of those false teachers is the real deal. Do not follow them.

It is implied in this verse that Christ taught His followers about following charismatic but false teachers at a prior time. He told them what to expect and how to tell the real from the counterfeit. The Apostle Paul said it this way in 2 Timothy 2:15: "Study to shew thyself approved unto God, a workman that needeth not to be ashamed, rightly dividing the word of truth." Long division might not have been a favorite exercise in math class, but the division spoken of here will go a long way to keep us from stumbling into the pitfalls of life.

Bank personnel do not bother looking at samples of counterfeit money. They constantly study the appearance of the real thing. When the bogus comes across their teller windows, they usually see it right away. We will not be smiling if the Lord personally has to tell us, "I told you so, but you didn't listen to Me."

And Simon he surnamed Peter

Maybe you have sung the favorite gospel song that goes like this: "There's a new name written down in glory, and it's mine, Oh yes, it's mine. . . ."

Several people in the Bible had name changes representing a change in their lives and their direction. Abraham and Sarah, Jacob, Daniel, and the Apostle Paul are among them. They all went on to serve God in ways they would never have dreamed.

Isaiah 62:2 ("And the Gentiles shall see thy righteousness, and all kings thy glory: and thou shalt be called by a new name, which the mouth of the LORD shall name.") mentions a name change for Israel at a future date when the King of Glory will reign on David's throne. Revelation 2:17 ("He that hath an ear, let him hear what the Spirit saith unto the churches; To him that overcometh will I give to eat of the hidden manna, and will give him a white stone, and in the stone a new name written, which no man knoweth saving he that receiveth it.") refers to a new name for those who have gone through the persecutions of this life at the hands of religion that opposes the truth of God's Word.

We don't know what our new name will be, but since we who are believers in the Lord are called His bride, we may have a hint. Let's illustrate it this way: John Jones and Gondolier Fafooffnyck meet, fall in love, and get married. From that day forward, she is (thankfully) no longer called Gondolier Fafooffnyck, but proudly shows her wedding ring to her friends and reminds them that she is now married to John and her name is now Mrs. John Jones.

Simon, the fisherman, is the first disciple mentioned in Mark 3, and the adding of a second name was immediate to his being called to follow the Lord. He became the obvious leader of the disciples as time went on. We often talk about Peter having the cleanest feet of the twelve because he had a habit of putting his foot in his mouth, but the reality is he became "rock" steady in his service for Christ in the days of the early church. (*Petros* is the Greek word for rock.)

What descriptive surname would the Lord give us? Faithful, truthful, lover of God, or undependable, lazy, self-serving.

Why not take a minute to consider what your new name might be and whether you might want to change it while there is still time to do so.

The sower soweth the word

The parable of the sower has been repeated countless times. The Word of God is the seed we have been given along with the task of sowing it.

If you have ever seen a modern farm, you may have seen the equipment used to mechanically place the seeds in the ground and cover them to the correct soil depth to assure growth to a mature plant, whether corn, wheat, or some other crop. When the Pilgrims came to North America nearly four hundred years ago, the Native Americans taught them to plant corn and fertilize each seed with a piece of dead fish to add nutrients to the soil and boost production.

In Bible times the farmer would "broadcast" the seed. That is, he would take a handful of grain and cast it across the field, move further down the row and repeat the process until the whole field had been sowed. Typically this would be done at the onset of the rainy season. One would presume he may have raked some soil over the seeds to keep them from being exposed to plunder by the birds.

Some of the seed would fall into an area where it could not germinate or where the birds, ever looking for a free meal, would get the seed before it could be protected. Other seed would land on rocks, which abound in the Holy Land. Possibly some would be in a crevice or depression where a little water would pool, allowing that seed to sprout, but it would soon die since there was no nutrition in the water alone. Even if it did survive a while, eventually the hot sun would dry up the water and the sprout would die.

If the farmer had prepared his land well, the seed would bring an abundant crop within its normal time, providing grain for sale, family, and livestock. Some of the fields would produce more than others, depending on the quality of the soil, the amount of water, and the care taken by the farmer.

The implication in this parable is that each believer in Jesus Christ is like a farmer. He has a bag full of seed, he has a field, and he has the commission to go into the world to preach the gospel. The first twenty verses of Mark 4 contain the parable and the explanation. The clear message is that we are responsible to sow, or tell, the gospel message to those who are in our field of influence.

The sower is the individual Christian. He sows the Word. Other farm workers water the fields; and still others may add fertilizer or pull up weeds. The seed we have is the best there is, so the potential for a bumper crop at harvest time is dependent on our faithfulness to the task we have been given.

We can call this, "Spiritual Farming 101." It is basic and easy to understand, just like most of Christ's parables—earthly stories with heavenly meanings.

Mark 6:42

*And they did all eat,
and were filled*

Try to imagine being a small boy on that Galilee hillside the day dinner was served by the disciples. Imagine it was your lunch everyone ate. While it is true a growing boy has a healthy appetite, it is a sure thing that he did not bring enough food in his lunch bag for thousands of his neighbors.

If anyone fully understood what really happened that day, it was that young boy. He willingly gave his lunch to Jesus and then watched the Lord reach into that bag again and again and again, taking more fish and more bread, and then some more, breaking more bite-sized pieces off than anyone could ever have believed possible.

What Jesus did to meet the physical hunger of five thousand men plus women and children, probably a total of fifteen thousand, even twenty thousand or more hungry people, was truly a miracle from a human standpoint. A greater miracle is what the Lord has done for any who have put their trust in Him. When He died on the cross, He died in our place, the just for the unjust. After being in the grave for three days and nights, He arose to live forevermore, making it possible for whosoever will ask for His forgiveness for sin to spend eternity in Heaven.

Back on that day, all of the people were fed and there was food left over. Today, all people can be saved from sin. Jesus is still satisfying the needs of any who will come to Him in faith, believing He will save them.

Mark 14:50

And they all forsook him, and fled

It is interesting to see the progression of these "One Liner" verses. While this is eight chapters later and has no direct connection to the previous one, we see reflected here a truism of life. As long as we are on the receiving end, we are more than happy to be close to the giver. When the going gets tough, man's natural tendency is to find something else to do, and to do it as far away as possible.

For three years, the disciples were at Jesus' side, and even though there were run-ins with the authorities from time to time, He had never been abandoned. This was a different situation. With the power of Rome behind him, the arrival of Judas on the scene scared the daylights out of the disciples, and they all ran. No doubt none of them ever expected to see Jesus alive again. It was great while it lasted, but now it was over!

The true test of friendship or love is whether one sticks by another in adversity. In our world of the twenty-first century, it is becoming more and more obvious that the fidelity, faith, and fortitude of true believers in Christ are being challenged. The encroachment of Islam in America, the threat of sha'aria law being parallel or supreme in our land, and the emboldening of those of any and all persuasions who are openly opposed to God's Word will separate the sheep from the goats, so to speak, and force believers to stand and fight or flee.

While the disciples, minus Judas, all returned to the Lord and were forgiven after He completed His redemption of man through His death, burial, and resurrection as victor over sin, death, and Hell, surely they had to face embarrassment or worse when they saw Him the next time.

It may be assumed that Peter was the first to be singled out since he was the outspoken leader, and probably the oldest of the disciples. After denying Christ three times, in John 21 he was asked if he truly loved the Lord three times. We are only told of Peter's conversation with the Lord at the end of the Gospel of John. The other disciples are spared from our having a bird's eye view of their red-faced meeting with the Lord. Imagine their joy, not just to see Jesus alive again, but to have been restored to full fellowship with Him. Surely the experience at the shore of Lake Galilee that morning made it clear to them not only Who Jesus was, but what their relationship to Him would be for the rest of their lives.

John 21:25 is the conclusion of John's gospel account: "And there are also many other things which Jesus did, the which, if they should be written every one, I suppose that even the world itself could not contain the books that should be written. Amen."

Obviously, each had received total forgiveness and restoration with the Lord, or NO books would have been written to tell us of His love for us. Each one of the disciples, with the exception of John, died a martyr for Christ. They willingly served the Lord no matter what came their way.

Reading John 21 would be a good thing to do as we contemplate the future and our dedication to serving the Lord in the last days of Grace. Surely the time of Tribulation about which the Lord warned cannot be too far in the future.

And they cried out again, Crucify him

Any one of us, if taking a minute or two to think, can remember a time in our lives when we were falsely accused. Those events are permanently etched in our minds and come back in great detail when we are reminded of them. It is human nature to have a mental "videotape" cued up and ready to replay at a second's notice of such events.

Humanly speaking, anyone who goes before a judge, even if accused of a crime for which he knows he is guilty, dreads the certain sound of the gavel and pronouncement of "Guilty!"

Humanly speaking, anyone who goes before a judge and knows he is not guilty, surely is shocked and dismayed to hear "Guilty!" Jesus was guilty of no crime worthy of death. There was nothing at all that could have been brought against Him in the legal sense. While there were no surprises for the Lord, Who knew the end from the beginning, we can imagine that His human nature must have cringed when the order to carry out the death sentence was handed down.

In John 6:37–40, Jesus said:

All that the Father giveth me shall come to me; and him that cometh to me I will in no wise cast out. For I came down from heaven, not to do mine own will, but the will of him that sent me. And this is the Father's will which hath sent me, that of all which he hath given me I should lose nothing, but should raise it up again at the last day. And this is the will of him that sent me, that every one which seeth the Son, and believeth on him, may have everlasting life: and I will raise him up at the last day.

How thankful we should be to know that our Lord lovingly came to endure the rejection and ultimate crucifixion to redeem us from sin. May we reflect that thankfulness in our faithful living to His glory!

Luke 11:3

Give us day by day our daily bread

As part of "The Lord's Prayer," better called the model prayer for Christ's disciples, this phrase is very familiar to most of the Christianized world. Given most of us like to eat, it may be the most often repeated portion of the prayer. Surely it exceeds "hallowed be Thy name . . ." and it would be safe to say it is more often thought of than "lead us not into temptation."

In our modern age we enjoy convenience stores and mind-boggling supermarkets loaded with every food and sub-variety imaginable at our fingertips. Even with many unemployed in America, most do not go hungry. We may not have eaten exactly what we wanted or as much as we may have wanted, but even the poorest among us fare well compared to those in many parts of the underdeveloped world.

Perhaps the Lord was reminding us that He is the source of all we have, and that He is all we need. At a moment's notice, our life circumstances can change. Tomorrow is not a guarantee, as our health could turn for the worse, our job could evaporate, or a disaster could take away everything we have. Even in the situations we have seen in recent years in New Orleans, Haiti, New Zealand, and Japan, where hurricanes, earthquakes, or tsunamis changed the conditions and quality of life in a matter of seconds, we can trust our gracious Lord to provide.

David said it this way: "Thou preparest a table before me in the presence of mine enemies: thou anointest my head with oil; my cup runneth over" (Psalm 23:5). In Psalm 65:9, he expands on the theme: "Thou visitest the earth, and waterest it: thou greatly enrichest it with the river of God, which is full of water: thou preparest them corn, when thou hast so provided for it."

Even in a faltering economy, the Lord can be trusted to meet our needs. It is important that we exercise care to be sure our needs are not confused with our wants!

Luke 17:32

Remember Lot's wife

If one were to travel in the Holy Land, in southern Israel's Negev Desert is found a rock formation that, with just a little bit of imagination, looks like a woman in a long dress. That formation is affectionately called "Lot's wife." Okay, you may need more than a little bit of imagination!

Perhaps you remember the Genesis account of Lot living in Sodom, one of the cities of the plain in the area of the southern end of the Dead Sea. The wickedness of that city and its sister city, Gomorrah, was so great that God singled it out for specific judgment. Whether that judgment was meteors, lightning strikes, or the divine equivalent of an atom bomb, we don't know. What we do know is that angels were dispatched to warn Lot and his family to flee and survive before the fire fell.

When they hesitated, the angels literally dragged them from the city. Genesis 19 has the account, and in 2 Peter 2, we read commentary on the event in verses 6–9:

> And turning the cities of Sodom and Gomorrha into ashes condemned them with an overthrow, making them an ensample unto those that after should live ungodly; and delivered just Lot, vexed with the filthy conversation of the wicked: (For that righteous man dwelling among them, in seeing and hearing, vexed his righteous soul from day to day with their unlawful deeds;) The Lord knoweth how to deliver the godly out of temptations, and to reserve the unjust unto the day of judgment to be punished.

Lot had compromised his testimony as a "just" man in God's sight, so much so that even his family scorned his warning to leave Sodom and were lost in the firestorm that fell.

Lot, Mrs. Lot, and the two young Misses Lot, escaped with little time to spare. Being warned not to look back, Mrs. Lot disobeyed, and in Genesis 19:26 we find she lagged behind Lot, and no doubt with the fear and compassion a mother has for her children, looked back, surely with tears streaming down her face.

Despite what some might argue, God was not being capricious or mean-spirited. His greatest desire is for His loved ones to be in close fellowship with Him. Mrs. Lot's heart was not Godward, but toward her children, home, and what she left behind. She had strayed from her love for the Lord, if indeed she was a believer in the true God and not one who grew up in, and clung to, the culture of Sodom. The principle here was spelled out by the Lord: "No man, having put his hand to the plow, and looking back, is fit for the kingdom of God" (Luke 9:62). Also in Psalm 37:3–5, "Trust in the LORD, and do good; so shalt thou dwell in the land, and verily thou shalt be fed. Delight thyself also in the LORD; and he shall give thee the desires of thine heart. Commit thy way unto the LORD; trust also in him; and he shall bring it to pass."

There is a lot to remember about Mrs. Lot. Maybe the most important lesson is found in Matthew 6:19–21: "Lay not up for yourselves treasures upon earth, where moth and rust doth corrupt, and where thieves break through and steal: But lay up for yourselves treasures in heaven, where neither moth nor rust doth corrupt, and where thieves do not break through nor steal: For where your treasure is, there will your heart be also."

One must wonder when and how God may once again rain down judgment on America and many other parts of the world where the sin of Sodom is prevalent. He called that activity wicked and an abomination then. We can be sure that He has not changed His mind after all these years, even though man has decided that what God calls sin is perfectly alright, and even preferable.

Remember Mrs. Lot. She had a lot of things that were important to her. It might be safe to assume the Lord God was nowhere near the top of that list.

Last of all the woman died also

The temptation to make a tongue-in-cheek remark at this point is nearly overwhelming. Ah, restraint! One's imagination can run wild considering the Sadducees' hypothetical situation of seven brothers all marrying the same woman. The Old Testament law was clear that a man should take his brother's wife to himself to have children in the name of the deceased. That poor woman! It is hard to imagine the Lord not having to suppress a smile or even a laugh as they laid out their improbable story in hopes of trying to ensnare Him.

One message we can take from this verse is: Life is short. Few of those who have lived for one hundred years or more have been heard to say, "Finally! I thought I would never die!" For most, the cry when at death's door is for a little more time.

The Lord turned this discussion to things eternal, reminding us that the really important things in life are not always what we think they are.

The day these words are being committed to the computer, the author had a conversation at a diner with a self-proclaimed atheist. We had already agreed to sharing the same conservative political views, but when he mentioned that he was a non-believer, and I commented that I was sorry to hear him say that, the conversation suddenly turned much darker.

While he firmly opposed them, he was clearly more tolerant to those of a "progressive" or communist/socialist political frame of mind than to someone who believed in a real and living God. The Sadducees probably would have welcomed my restaurant acquaintance among them as another who understood many of the important things, but like them, missed out on some of the most important things in all of life, namely, those things that pertain to an eternity that truly lasts forever in either Heaven or Hell.

Luke 20:43

Till I make thine enemies thy footstool

This snippet of the narrative needs context, so to Luke 20:41–47 we go: "And he said unto them, How say they that Christ is David's son? And David himself saith in the book of Psalms, The Lord said unto my Lord, Sit thou on my right hand, Till I make thine enemies thy footstool. David therefore calleth him Lord, how is he then his son? Then in the audience of all the people he said unto his disciples, Beware of the scribes, which desire to walk in long robes, and love greetings in the markets, and the highest seats in the synagogues, and the chief rooms at feasts; Which devour widows' houses, and for a show make long prayers: the same shall receive greater damnation."

Our Lord seldom needed to do much to make the scribes and Pharisees look foolish. They did most of the heavy work themselves. They wanted nothing more than to trip Jesus on His own words or to trap Him in some area of the law. The words of David here seem to form a riddle. How could the Lord address the Lord when He was both his lord and his son?

Because the scripture is complete, we know the answer. David's son many generations later would be the one who would become the Savior and Lord of all, including David.

While the religious leaders of the day were in a huddle trying to figure out an answer, the Lord Jesus warned all within hearing of their leaders' love of being showered with attention and adoration, how that they would dress so anyone would know who they were and parade around in public so people would show them deference and honor. Their pride had destroyed their ministry and effectiveness. Their love of money and public recognition rather than their humility and service had set them up to be condemned by the Lord.

In Matthew 20 and Mark 10, Jesus reprimanded James, John, and their mother for thinking they were important, telling them, "but whosoever will be great among you, shall be your minister: And whosoever of you will be the chiefest, shall be servant of all. For even the Son of man came not to be ministered unto, but to minister, and to give his life a ransom for many" (Mark 10:43–45).

One wonders what He might say to some of the religious leaders of today who, with the aid of radio and television, have received such fame and fortune in our time. If Christ did not come to earth to be served, but to serve, how much more should we humbly serve Him?

There are many in the world today who are the enemies of the gospel and more specifically, enemies of Jesus Christ. While they may seem to have freedom to do their damage now, they will stand before the same Lord they hate to be judged and sentenced to eternal separation from Him. Truly the Lord's enemies will be crushed under His feet.

Luke 21:13

And it shall turn to you for a testimony

We find this verse in the midst of what we call "The Olivet Discourse." This teaching is where Christ warned His disciples then, and all those who have since read the account, of the future days before He returns in glory with His saints to rule and reign on earth.

Today's news is full of confirmation of what He told His disciples on the Mount of Olives shortly before His arrest and crucifixion. The world is becoming increasingly dangerous and less friendly toward one who proclaims faith in Jesus Christ. In many parts of the world, people have laid down their lives or rotted in prisons because they would not renounce their faith in Christ or keep silent in their witness. The persecution to which the Lord was referring is not limited to the Tribulation period. It has been happening since His days on earth. It will only get worse as the days approach for His return.

At some point in time, we may find ourselves forced to give account of our faith, and the result of our answer could determine whether we live or die.

Luke 21:14–17 serves as legal counsel to us: "Settle it therefore in your hearts, not to meditate before what ye shall answer: For I will give you a mouth and wisdom, which all your adversaries shall not be able to gainsay nor resist. And ye shall be betrayed both by parents, and brethren, and kinsfolks, and friends; and some of you shall they cause to be put to death. And ye shall be hated of all men for my name's sake."

In the United States, where we have enjoyed freedom of religion since the founding of our Republic, we are now seeing the foreshadows of the type of persecution mentioned here. Political winds are shifting. Our elected leaders are turning their backs on the laws and practices that have guided our nation to be the blessing to the rest of the world that it has been. The politically expedient and politically correct things to do to find the favor of some group have superceded everything from our classic classroom texts to the practice of law in the courts.

When the world turns to you or to me for a testimony, what will we say?

Luke 21:19

In your patience possess ye your souls

This verse follows closely the previous one. When the promised persecution comes, flying off the handle or becoming aggressive and hate-filled will accomplish nothing. First Peter 3:4 refers to a meek and quiet spirit, which is in the sight of God of great price.

We may be hated by all of the ungodly because we claim the name of the Lord Jesus Christ. However, based on God's Word, no matter what man does to us, God not only is in control, but He will get the ultimate glory and we will rule and reign with Him in the future.

If we have fully trusted Him for our salvation, even in the darkest of days to come, we can look forward to the reward and joy of being in His presence for all eternity!

Luke 24:8

And they remembered his words

At one time or another, everyone has said something like, "Of course, I remember now!" How easy it is to forget important things, especially when we are under pressure from work, family, or whatever else, only to suddenly be brought back to reality by remembering something we had been told or had seen.

Grief and despair had overwhelmed Christ's followers. He had given them so much hope and joy when He walked with them. Then the unthinkable happened. The most gentle person who had ever walked on earth had been falsely accused, tried in an illegal court, and sentenced to death. Satanically orchestrated, the events proceeded until He was nailed to a cross like a common criminal and allowed to die.

"What are we to do now?"

It was the women who were close to the Lord who put their grief into action. Carrying the spices and wrapping cloths used to prepare a body for burial according to the Jewish customs of the day, they went to the tomb. The Roman guards had been posted to insure that no one would steal the body of the Lord, and then make the claim that He had risen from the dead. Surely the women must have found it curious that the guards were gone when they arrived; even more strange, the body was gone, too. How? Why? Who?

If the last few days had not been bizarre enough, they next saw two angels who gave them the good news that Jesus had arisen from the dead.

It was then they remembered His words. He had taught that He would be taken by the hands of cruel men and put to death, but would arise again the third day. What had at the time gone over their heads now sank in. He really meant it; and what's more, He had done it!

Oh, it wasn't that they didn't believe Him; surely He would never lie to them, but dead people who were placed in a grave never escaped! Did they?

Jesus just had!

All He had taught suddenly had a whole new meaning. In today's vernacular, we would say, Jesus had put His money where His mouth was. He had fulfilled the wildest promise ever made to that day. In Mark 8, Jesus had just asked the disciples who they thought he really was. Peter made the great statement: "Thou art the Christ." Peter told the Lord that he believed and trusted that He was the long-promised Messiah of Israel. In His response, Jesus in verse 31 ". . . began to teach them, that the Son of man must suffer many things, and be rejected of the elders, and of the chief priests, and scribes, and be killed, and after three days rise again."

That was the beginning of a large multitude who believed His Word and who became His followers from that day to this. We remember His words, and realize they are the source of our salvation and eternal life.

Luke 24:43

*And he took it, and did eat
before them*

After a funeral, it is often the custom for friends and family to gather at the family homestead, a restaurant, or at a church fellowship hall and share a meal together. Many stories are told of people's experiences with the departed friend or loved one. There will be many laughs and most likely as many tears. When the group finally disperses, all will agree they know more about the one who has died than they did before.

This verse is in the middle of a meal after a funeral. Not quite the same kind, to be sure, since the departed had returned and was with them at the table. Just a few minutes prior, Jesus' friends and followers were moping around, their faces downcast, or doubting the stories they were beginning to hear that Jesus had appeared to some of them. Hallucinations! Wishful thinking. Dreams!

Alive? Come on, get real! That doesn't happen.

One blink of an eye later, there was Jesus in the room with them. What a shock that must have been! Surely it must have been mass delusion. This wasn't real. The doors were locked, and besides, He had been put in the grave three days before.

After an invitation to touch Him, examine His wounds, and see that He was real, He did something that would serve as the "acid test." He asked for something to eat. A ghost would not eat. Most likely, the average person would think that if a ghost might try to eat something, it

[37]

would end up falling on the floor, since there is no bodily substance to a spirit.

Jesus was not a ghost; He was the victorious, living God who was honoring them by revealing Himself to them in His glorified body. They were the first of countless millions who have to this time placed their trust in Him. They had the opportunity to see Him firsthand, we believe based on the testimony of those who were there without having the experience of physically touching Him or being eyewitnesses to His resurrection.

In John 20:29 is the account of a week later when Jesus spoke to "doubting" Thomas: "Jesus saith unto him, Thomas, because thou hast seen me, thou hast believed: blessed are they that have not seen, and yet have believed." We are among those so blessed. Best of all, we will see Him face to face some day, maybe very soon!

Luke 24:48

And ye are witnesses of these things

Let's assume you don't know what "these things" are.

In the short space of about three and a half years, Jesus came out of small town obscurity, preached throughout the Galilee, did the extraordinary—if not impossible—and was crucified. Just when everyone thought it was all over and prepared to go back home to live a normal life, He did the impossible. He arose from the dead.

Within minutes of this reminder to His friends and followers recorded in this "One Liner," He lifted off from the surface of the earth and went back to Heaven with the promise that He would return later for those who love Him. While we are in the mood to assume things, let's assume something else: YOU were there and saw it all. Now, do you think you could keep your mouth shut? Hardly. Would you have gone back to your home and job to live your life as normal?

Most of the disciples became martyrs. Only John lived to an old age, but not before he had been boiled in oil, to name just one thing done to him by Imperial Rome. No, it was not the easy life for them. You want witnesses? There are none better when you consider they stuck to their story knowing full well they were in line for martyrdom. If Jesus was not real, had not done the miracles, and if He had not risen from the grave in triumph, don't think for one minute they would have stood by the Lord when the persecution came. To be sure, if it all was a made up story, a lie, some of them—most of them—would have changed their story and we would have historical records of the recanting of their original account. Instead, books like *Foxe's Book of Marytrs* and others written more recently tell of those who would not bow and would not bend, but if necessary, would burn at the stake rather than renounce the One Who died for their sins. He was that real to them.

Few people will die for a lie. The disciples were sold out for the Lord because they knew He was real. At this late date in history, we are not eyewitnesses, nor are any others who are alive today. However, we are intended to be witnesses, giving testimony to His saving grace and power in our lives. "But ye shall receive power, after that the Holy Ghost is come upon you: and ye shall be witnesses unto me both in Jerusalem, and in all Judaea, and in Samaria, and unto the uttermost part of the earth. (Acts 1:8).

In a court of law, the responsibility of a witness is to tell what he has seen or experienced, and knows to be true. Christ's power, promised to us moments before He left this earth, is ours. All we need do is prayerfully trust Him to give us the words to say when we are willing to represent Him in our everyday lives.

An incredible number of American churches are closing their doors. Many have become mosques, museums, or rotting corpses of buildings, where at one time in the past, they had made a difference in the lives of those in the community. They have lost their mission, their vision, and their power.

The Lord said, "Ye SHALL be witnesses. . . ." Being shy is not a viable excuse. Witnessing is part of our job description. Angels don't spread the gospel. While it is true that most people would rather watch football, play golf, or sleep in on Sunday morning than to go to church, what might happen if you went out of your comfort zone on a Saturday and knocked on some doors in your part of town and invited your neighbors or strangers to go to church with you? Instead of expecting someone else to do it, offer to give a ride to someone who needs one. Most cars that fill the church parking spaces come in at least half empty.

It is not surprising that the churches that are growing and reaching souls for the Savior are those with an active door-to-door witnessing program. Some of our friends at churches down the street believe God will do all that is needed to reach those He intends to save and that they don't need to actively witness for Him. They have missed the clear command. The words of Christ in Mark 16:15 are clear and simple: "Go ye into all the world, and preach the gospel to every creature."

John 2:21

But he spake of the temple of his body

It is much too easy to misunderstand someone. They knew what they were thinking as they spoke, but maybe they didn't express themselves well. In this case, Jesus was misunderstood because, even if He had clearly spoken about what He meant, He still would not have been understood by most in His audience.

Checking the background of this verse will bring some clarity. For turning it into a bazaar, Jesus had just chased the money changers from the temple court, fulfilling Psalm 69:9, which says, "For the zeal of thine house hath eaten me up. . . ." The temple precincts had been turned into a currency exchange since the money of the pagan nations was considered unclean and not welcome at the temple. If you had come a distance with the currency of your nation, you went to the exchange to get the accepted money for temple giving. Anyone who has traveled abroad knows the routine. In effect, it had become a racket, with just a little more of the money going into the pockets of the bankers than it should have.

Mark 11:15–18 gives the account:

> And they come to Jerusalem: and Jesus went into the temple, and began to cast out them that sold and bought in the temple, and overthrew the tables of the moneychangers, and the seats of them that sold doves; And would not suffer that any man should carry any vessel

through the temple. And he taught, saying unto them, Is it not written, My house shall be called of all nations the house of prayer? but
ye have made it a den of thieves. And the scribes and chief priests
heard it, and sought how they might destroy him: for they feared him,
because all the people was astonished at his doctrine.

Another version of this event, including this verse, is in John 2:13–21:

And the Jews' passover was at hand, and Jesus went up to Jerusalem,
And found in the temple those that sold oxen and sheep and doves,
and the changers of money sitting: And when he had made a scourge
of small cords, he drove them all out of the temple, and the sheep,
and the oxen; and poured out the changers' money, and overthrew
the tables; And said unto them that sold doves, Take these things
hence; make not my Father's house an house of merchandise. And
his disciples remembered that it was written, The zeal of thine house
hath eaten me up. Then answered the Jews and said unto him, What
sign showest thou unto us, seeing that thou doest these things? Jesus
answered and said unto them, Destroy this temple, and in three days I
will raise it up. Then said the Jews, Forty and six years was this temple
in building, and wilt thou rear it up in three days? But he spake of the
temple of his body.

When He claimed the temple as His Father's house, He really pushed
the hot buttons of the religious leaders.

Who did He think He was to claim that kind of authority over them?
After all, they were the leaders of the day! They were the priests in the
temple of God! And surely, for calling God His father, Jesus was being
just a little bit too forward, wasn't He? When they asked for a sign of
His authority, He told them, "Destroy this temple, and in three days I
will raise it up."

They made a natural mistake at this point. They were not His serious followers, but hung around occasionally hoping to hear Him say
something they could use against Him. Well! This was just what they
had been waiting for! He just proved to their thinking that He was a
crackpot. Since so many followed Him, He was a dangerous crackpot,
for sure.

The building project known as the Herodian temple had been going on for decades. It was a marvel to see. You can almost hear the sneer in their voices and see the snickers on the faces of the leaders of the temple when they heard His claim. He had said some radical things before, and when confronting these over-inflated leaders, He had gained a following among the ordinary folks at their expense by calling them hypocrites instead of showing them the respect they felt they were due, but this topped everything. Do what? Rebuild what? In how long? Ha! Right!

Later, our Lord was crucified through the manipulations, no doubt, of some of those same religious leaders, and after three days and three nights, He had risen triumphantly from the dead and is alive forevermore. The temple building would be destroyed by the Roman forces led by Titus Vespatian about forty years later in A.D. 70. That temple is yet to be restored, but Jesus kept His promise, even though it was misunderstood by many.

John 4:4

And he must needs go through Samaria

It would be easy to miss the fact that this verse contains one of the most beautiful of the "One Liners." God Himself was walking the dusty roads of Judea, but found it necessary to go into Samaria. It is important to remember that the Samaritans were half-breeds and were held in very low regard by the Jews. There was virtually no association between the two groups.

Invading nations, when conquering another nation, would export some of the citizens of that country to another area they controlled. They would import some of the subjects of yet another area to fill the void. The result of this clever migration shell game, or forced intermixing of nationalities, would be a lack of adhesion between the people. Diverse people groups who cannot agree on much would isolate themselves from those who were not like them and would have a hard time becoming strong enough to become a threat to their conquerors. It is the same today. We are seeing this in several parts of the world as "social engineers" are trying to bring about drastic changes in the world order.

Jews, by and large, "had no dealings with the Samaritans." To maintain the purity of their religion and bloodlines, they kept to themselves. The Samaritans, half Jewish and half who knows what else, were not Jewish enough, and therefore, they qualified to be avoided.

Yet, we read that Jesus HAD to go through Samaria.

The story that follows is one of the greatest love stories in all of history. No, not the gushy, soap opera kind of love. This is the deep love of the Savior for one in need of being saved. It is a story that gives hope to many who would consider themselves hopeless.

We find the Lord alone by the side of a well in the middle of the day. No one came to the well at that hour. It was too hot, the flocks had already been watered, the laundry was already drying, and the well would be visited by only a very few until evening. Here was Jesus.

By and by, a woman—a Samaritan woman, at that—came to the well. This was her time to come to the well so she could avoid unwanted contact with the other women of the town. She had a reputation—a bad one. Normally, neither the woman nor Jesus would have spoken to the other, but Jesus asked her for a drink. She had a bucket, so she could meet His need, but she didn't realize how empty her bucket was nor how great was her personal need, even as she brought it dripping up from the depths of the well to satisfy the Lord's thirst.

In their brief conversation, she found that Jesus could give her a kind of water of which she had never dreamed. The water of life. Eternal life. She knew of the anticipated Jewish Messiah, but this was the day she met Him face to face.

John 4:39–42, the end of the story, reveals the results of a simple visit from God, wrapped in human flesh: "And many of the Samaritans of that city believed on him for the saying of the woman, which testified, He told me all that ever I did. So when the Samaritans were come unto him, they besought him that he would tarry with them: and he abode there two days. And many more believed because of his own word; And said unto the woman, Now we believe, not because of thy saying: for we have heard him ourselves, and know that this is indeed the Christ, the Saviour of the world."

In John 4:35, Jesus' message to His disciples was: "Lift up your eyes, and look on the fields; for they are white already to harvest." He knew this woman needed His water more than He needed hers. He knows what our neighbors, family, and friends need, too. They need the water of life. So do the people that are outside of our comfort zone. He must needs go through Samaria. Where must we go to fulfill our responsibility to the "Great Commission" to take the gospel to every creature?

John 11:35

Jesus wept

This is the shortest verse in the text of the King James Bible. To some degree, it is also the springboard verse resulting in this complete devotional effort.

Some years ago when this writer was a teenager, our small church had a Sunday school teacher who invested heavily in the lives of his charges. Warren Bossert was his name. He had a love for the most unlovable people in the world: junior high school boys. Every month we had a "class meeting." We would be rounded up for a few hours at the home of one of the boys where we would discuss the things we wanted to do, activities we wanted to have, have a devotional time, and, of course, eat—something junior high boys do very well.

One memorable evening, one of our number, Hank by name, was in a cantankerous mood that turned the tables on him. Mr. Bossert surprised him at devotion time, and said, "Hank, if you think you have something to say, why don't you teach the Bible study tonight?"

On many occasions prior, when someone was asked to give a favorite scripture verse, John 11:35 would often be quoted. No one had to strain their brain to memorize that verse! It was easy to fall back on it if not prepared with another.

Hank, knowing his bluff had been called, accepted the challenge and gave a brief devotional on the verse. Actually, when he realized he really had to teach a Bible lesson, he got serious, and gave us a good summary of the reason for the verse.

And just what is the message of this verse? Jesus was God, but while on the earth, He was also very human. The theologians have a twenty-five dollar word for it: "The Hypostatic Union." He is the God-Man—totally God and totally man at the same time. In human terms, it is not possible to explain, but there are a lot of things in this life and even more about God that we cannot explain.

When Jesus' close friend Lazarus died, and when He saw the level of grief expressed by those who loved him, Jesus was moved with compassion so much that the emotions present in His human nature poured out in tears.

Hebrews 4:14–16 gives a peek into His nature: "Seeing then that we have a great high priest, that is passed into the heavens, Jesus the Son of God, let us hold fast our profession. For we have not an high priest which cannot be touched with the feeling of our infirmities; but was in all points tempted like as we are, yet without sin. Let us therefore come boldly unto the throne of grace, that we may obtain mercy, and find grace to help in time of need."

Whatever our needs may be, He knows what they are and how to meet them. He has experienced all the emotions and temptations that we humans do, but did not fall to sin. What a comfort it is that He knows us, understands us, and has made provision for our sinful natural condition that we can know the forgiveness of the holy God of the universe because He became us so that we might live with Him for all eternity.

John 16:9

Of sin, because they believe not on me

John 16:7–11 is the context for this verse. "It is expedient for you that I go away: for if I go not away, the Comforter will not come unto you; but if I depart, I will send him unto you. And when he is come, he will reprove the world of sin, and of righteousness, and of judgment: Of sin, because they believe not on me; Of righteousness, because I go to my Father, and ye see me no more; Of judgment, because the prince of this world is judged."

We often think of one who gives reproof as being a self-righteous, finger-wagging, unforgiving older person with a wart at the end of his nose. When it comes to the Comforter Christ promised to send—the Holy Spirit—that visual concept could not be farther from the truth. Today's society has lost almost all sense of propriety, morals, truth, decency, and much more. The average person today sees little wrong with breaking any or all of the Ten Commandments, or any other law known to man. By comparison, a true believer in Jesus Christ has the indwelling Holy Spirit—the Comforter—who is the still small voice to guide, remind, or chastise when doing wrong. The Third Person of the Trinity is the conscience, if you will, but much more than the common concept of conscience. He is the one who has been called alongside us to help us through life. The still small voice that will guide us into all truth.

After Christ returned to Heaven, the Holy Spirit came and has been with Christians ever since, and He is very effective in His ministry. A believer has a hard time getting away with anything wrong since his conscience will bother him until the sin is confessed. While not having the believer's direct ministry of the Holy Spirit, the unbeliever is affected by the Holy Spirit, too, if only indirectly when seeing a true Christian act as he should.

The unsaved person sins by natural course. He was born in sin, lives in sin, and will die in his sins if he never places his trust in the finished work of Calvary, where Christ died and paid for the sins of all. Even the unsaved person knows when he is doing wrong. He or she is convicted in his own conscience by the Holy Spirit, whose work is to point people to Christ, "because they believe not. . . ."

No one comes to Christ without the ministry of the Holy Spirit. His primary job is to point people to Christ. His constant ministry is stated in verses 13 and 14: "Howbeit when he, the Spirit of truth, is come, he will guide you into all truth: for he shall not speak of himself; but whatsoever he shall hear, that shall he speak: and he will show you things to come. He shall glorify me: for he shall receive of mine, and shall show it unto you."

If you know the truth, it shall make you free, and you know the truth because you were guided and taught it by the Holy Spirit of God, the third person of the Trinity.

Acts 8:8

And there was great joy in that city

When a revival breaks out in a city, it is truly cause for great joy. Joy is much more than happiness. Happiness can come and go. We get a present, a raise, a new baby in the family, a pat on the back, and we are happy. Joy is much deeper. Joy can be compared to a glass being filled at the kitchen sink's tap when someone forgets to turn off the flow of the water. The glass fills to the top, and having no more room to hold more, it starts to overflow.

Acts 8:5-8 gives insight to this verse: "Then Philip went down to the city of Samaria, and preached Christ unto them. And the people with one accord gave heed unto those things which Philip spake, hearing and seeing the miracles which he did. For unclean spirits, crying with loud voice, came out of many that were possessed with them: and many taken with palsies, and that were lame, were healed. And there was great joy in that city."

Philip was one of the first Christian evangelists. By this time in history, the gospel was being ministered to more than just the Jews, and that brought Philip to Samaria. The Old Testament understanding of God was within the Jewish nationality. Now, instead of being outsiders to the grace of God, all people groups were included in Christ's gracious invitation to "Come unto me. . . ."

Philip preached, the people listened, the Holy Spirit convicted, and one by one, people were delivered from their sins and infirmities. The results were irrefutable and the snowball effect continued until the whole city was irreversibly changed.

There was great joy in that city! When people see the results of the Christ-filled life in others, they will respond. May our lives be so clearly reflective of Jesus Christ that not only will people give heed to what is said, but that they will come to know the joy of sins forgiven, a personal relationship with the Creator-God and the hope of eternal life in Heaven.

Walking clean in the Spirit of God enables one to be like that over-flowing glass that results in people being drawn to the Savior and experiencing great joy.

Acts 17:33

*So Paul departed
from among them*

Athens, Greece, is one of those places on the "Must Visit!" list. With the Parthenon, the Acropolis, and so much ancient history, it has become iconic for a traveler or lover of antiquities. Back in the days of Athens' glory entered Paul, the great missionary statesman of the first century. He took the guided tour and discovered the city was wholly given to idolatry (Acts 17:16).

When he spoke to the religious and city elite, they thought he had brought some strange doctrine to offer them. The news of Christ and His resurrection from the dead was foreign to the Athenians, and the concept that all men could have eternal life was truly a new idea to them. Long before the advent of talk radio, the people of Athens had turned talk for talk's sake into an art form, so they asked Paul to tell them more. On Mars Hill, the meeting place and center of their pagan worship, Paul couldn't help seeing the altars to their many gods; but for Paul, the one that stood out from the rest was the one with the inscription, "To the Unknown God." The people of Athens wanted to be sure they didn't forget anyone or offend some god they hadn't heard of before, so this altar was erected and doubtlessly venerated by many, just to be sure they had their bases covered.

Pointing to that altar, "Let me tell you about Him," Paul said.

When he preached Christ to them, and got to the part about His rising from the grave, victorious over death, something happened that happens even today. Many men educated in the wisdom of the world find it easier to turn their backs on God's Word at this point in the story than to continue the discussion or investigation into the truth of the Bible.

In 1 Corinthians 1:18–25, Paul laid out the case against the educated mind that insists on seeing everything with the eye or touching it with the hand:

> For the preaching of the cross is to them that perish foolishness; but unto us which are saved it is the power of God. For it is written, I will destroy the wisdom of the wise, and will bring to nothing the understanding of the prudent. Where is the wise? where is the scribe? where is the disputer of this world? hath not God made foolish the wisdom of this world? For after that in the wisdom of God the world by wisdom knew not God, it pleased God by the foolishness of preaching to save them that believe. For the Jews require a sign, and the Greeks seek after wisdom: But we preach Christ crucified, unto the Jews a stumblingblock, and unto the Greeks foolishness; But unto them which are called, both Jews and Greeks, Christ the power of God, and the wisdom of God. Because the foolishness of God is wiser than men; and the weakness of God is stronger than men.

So many people today, as then, are educated too much! They can accept nothing by faith. Back in Athens, Paul's preaching earned mixed reviews. Some scoffed at him for talking about something so ridiculous as someone arising from the dead, but others decided to hear him again at a later date.

There was a third group. These are they who accepted the message Paul preached and put their trust in Christ. Most likely in numbers they were a smaller group than the other two, but their names are written in the Lamb's Book of Life.

Very soon after this, Paul left Athens for Corinth. Those who rejected Paul's message were not affected by his departure; they didn't care. If those who postponed making their decision ever thought of Paul again, they were too late; he was gone.

This is a perfect picture of the people who surround us in the world today. Some scoff and walk away. Others scratch their heads and say, "That's interesting. Let me think about it . . ." while others simply say, "God, be merciful to me, a sinner."

In 2 Corinthians 6:1–2, the imploring evangelist Paul said, "We then, . . . beseech you also that ye receive not the grace of God in vain. (For he saith, I have heard thee in a time accepted, and in the day of salvation have I succoured [helped] thee: behold, now is the accepted time; behold, now is the day of salvation.)"

The likelihood is strong that those who scoffed and those who postponed accepting God's offer of grace are now awaiting final sentencing to a hopeless eternity in the lake of fire. God offers opportunity, but He may not offer it more than once. It is a limited time offer. If you, reader, have never put your faith in Jesus Christ as your Savior from your sins, don't delay. He died not because He had sinned or broken the law. Just the opposite, "For Christ also hath once suffered for sins, the just for the unjust, that he might bring us to God, being put to death in the flesh, but quickened [made alive again] by the Spirit . . ." (1 Peter 3:18).

And he wrote a letter after this manner

There are very few passages of scripture that were written by unbelievers or non-Jews. The letter that follows is one of them. Paul is being held prisoner because he dared to preach in the name of Jesus. This angered more than forty men so much, they bound themselves with an oath that they would neither eat or drink until they had killed Paul.

We know little about Paul's family. We do learn in this chapter of Acts that he had a sister who had a son. Paul's nephew overheard what was being plotted and told Paul. No doubt, it was Paul's clear testimony and right living that gave him favor with the Roman soldiers assigned to him. Paul told his nephew to tell the centurion of the plot, and the centurion told his chief captain, Claudius Lysias. Because of the respect Paul had earned among the Roman legion that was guarding him, his nephew ended up foiling the plot by being a faithful witness of what he had seen and heard. The result of the report he gave was that Paul's life was saved, as surely were those of several of the soldiers.

Claudius Lysias is not a name many of us would remember. More than likely, he took his stylus and opened the hinged box that had two wax pages that had been melted to make a smooth surface at the bottom of the two open sections and wrote what the Holy Spirit has preserved in Acts 23:26–30:

> Claudius Lysias unto the most excellent governor Felix sendeth greeting. This man was taken of the Jews, and should have been killed of them: then came I with an army, and rescued him, having understood

that he was a Roman. And when I would have known the cause wherefore they accused him, I brought him forth into their council: Whom I perceived to be accused of questions of their law, but to have nothing laid to his charge worthy of death or of bonds. And when it was told me how that the Jews laid wait for the man, I sent straightway to thee, and gave commandment to his accusers also to say before thee what they had against him. Farewell.

Early the next morning, a virtual army set out under cover of darkness. Paul was safely surrounded by some four hundred and seventy horse-mounted and foot soldiers. Their destination was Caesarea Maritima on the Mediterranean coast to the north. It was here that Herod, the builder-king, had a coastal fortress, palace, vacation hideaway, and seaport. The extensive ruins of it still visible today are impressive. What it was then, we can only begin to imagine. It was here that Paul would spend considerable time before the Lord's promise to him in Acts 23:11 would come true: "Be of good cheer, Paul: for as thou hast testified of me in Jerusalem, so must thou bear witness also at Rome."

A nephew, a trusting chief captain, and a pagan ruler worked together to ensure a promise from God would come to pass. One has to wonder if any of those forty or so men died of starvation!

Romans 3:15

Their feet are swift to shed blood

Romans 3:16

Destruction and misery are in their ways

Romans 3:18

There is no fear of God before their eyes

Three verses in rapid succession are before us. The Apostle Paul must have been a formidable foe on the debate team in high school. He is a master of logical argument. The question he is debating at this point is the value of being circumcised versus not being circumcised. Obviously, the Jews of his day thought it was very important, as it was a sign God had given as far back as Abraham to separate His chosen people from the rest of the world. At the center of his argument is the case for there being no difference between Jew and gentile, since both are sinners in light of the righteousness of a thrice-holy God.

Romans 3:9–20 is at the center of the case, and in the center of this passage are our "One Liners":

> What then? are we better than they? No, in no wise: for we have be-
> fore proved both Jews and Gentiles, that they are all under sin; As it is

written, There is none righteous, no, not one: There is none that understandeth, there is none that seeketh after God. They are all gone out of the way, they are together become unprofitable; there is none that doeth good, no, not one. Their throat is an open sepulchre; with their tongues they have used deceit; the poison of asps is under their lips: Whose mouth is full of cursing and bitterness: Their feet are swift to shed blood: Destruction and misery are in their ways: And the way of peace have they not known: There is no fear of God before their eyes. Now we know that what things soever the law saith, it saith to them who are under the law: that every mouth may be stopped, and all the world may become guilty before God. Therefore by the deeds of the law there shall no flesh be justified in his sight: for by the law is the knowledge of sin.

In a legal case before judge and jury, many facts need to be confirmed before the case is clearly defined and guilt or innocence is determined. God had already set down in His Word enough definitions of sin as to encompass everyone who ever lived. While one may not have murdered, he lied. Gotcha! Adultery may not be on your conscience, but surely you remember when you were a child, taking an irresistibly warm cookie when you knew you weren't supposed to. Gotcha! The list of "gotcha's" here is sufficiently comprehensive that every mouth would be stopped. Paul is referring to all of humanity as he lays down his case. The "they," "their," "every," and "all" in this passage include everyone who has ever lived. This is not a Jew versus the rest of the world issue. Each of us has offended in some area or another. An honest look at the list would have any of us forced to admit to guilt for several things so that there shall no flesh be justified in his sight.

Case closed!

Let not then your good be evil spoken of

Don't do the right thing the wrong way. Easily said. Hard to do. Sometimes our motives are difficult to hide, and while we may do something good, the ulterior motive behind the deed may negate any positive effect it may have.

It is hard enough to live a life that glorifies the Lord. Add to that not being a stumbling block to those who see us on the job or in the neighborhood, and hard approaches impossible. While, as verse 14 says, we will all stand before God to give account of our lives at some future day, today we stand before our neighbors, family, and friends.

If we have been faithful in our witness to them, the first time we slip, the first time we say something they feel is inappropriate for someone who has reached "perfection" as they may try to say, we have blown our testimony. We are held to a different standard once we separate ourselves from the cursing, drinking, gambling crowd. That is especially true if we were part of that lifestyle B.C.—Before Christ. Once we are deemed to be "holier than thou," we are made of fragile pottery that will break to thousands of pieces when we fall.

It would be so much easier if we did achieve sinless perfection when we accept Christ as Savior, but that doesn't happen.

Paul is using the example of a kosher diet to illustrate his point. If a Jewish person who follows a kosher diet were to eat a ham sandwich, he would be considered unclean. His standing in the community would be severely compromised if it were to become a regular way of life for him to eat ham, shrimp, cheeseburgers, and many of the other things banned in the Jewish kosher dietary laws.

By the same manner, those in the world will be quick to point to a witnessing Christian who has done something even the unsaved recognize as wrong. A testimony goes down the drain very easily. While the glitterati of Hollywood or the famous of music, sports, or television can do almost anything and still see their ratings go up, a Christian is held to a higher standard.

That may be thought of as being unfair, but the reality is we answer not to the general public, but to Almighty God. He gave His best for us. We owe Him our best. Let us guard our walk, our talk, and those around us so that there will be no room for our good to be evil spoken of.

Greet Amplias my beloved in the Lord

Who in the world was Amplias? We don't know anything more about him than is found in this verse.

When we look at the major characters in God's Word, names like Adam, Noah, Abraham, Isaac, Jacob, Joseph, David, Daniel, Isaiah, Paul, and Peter are only a few on the rather long list that could be created with no effort.

Here, in a few verses, two dozen people are mentioned. Most of them, like Amplias, are unknown to history and to us, but to Paul and the Lord they were important. Did God allow Paul an extra minute of writing time to list personal friends and helpers to his ministry, or were these names fully part of the inspiration of the scripture?

Second Timothy 3:16–17 answers the question: "All scripture is given by inspiration of God, and is profitable for doctrine, for reproof, for correction, for instruction in righteousness: That the man of God may be perfect, throughly furnished unto all good works."

If nothing else, from these verses we learn that God sees the little guy. He cares about the little guy. He remembers the little guy. Amplias may have been a little guy by man's standards, but Paul esteemed him highly enough to call him one he loved in the Lord.

What do we need to do to be on the list of God's beloved? Luke's gospel gives the answer: "He that is faithful in that which is least is faithful also in much: and he that is unjust in the least is unjust also in much" (Luke 16:10).

If nothing else, Paul's commendatory mention of Amplias was surely an encouragement to him and others in Rome. They now knew that Paul, their mentor and friend, appreciated whatever it was that had been done on his behalf. They were not taken for granted. It also reveals that God doesn't see anyone who is faithful to Him as insignificant.

Since God sees our actions as well as our hearts, He knows what we have done, and He knows what we would do if we could. Amplias most likely had a servant's heart, and his faithful service to Paul and to the Lord did not go unnoticed. He earned a place in God's roll call of honor, and we can, too. The key is faithfulness.

Have we not power to eat and to drink?

In Paul's day, idolatry was common among the nations of the Mediterranean, and food offerings would be made to pagan idols. People would bring a piece of meat, some grain, a flagon of wine, or whatever they had and present it to their false god, seeking favor from it. After it had been presented, the priests of the pagan temples would eat or use what they wanted, but the rest would be sold to the merchants in the shambles, or open air markets of the town. They in turn would sell the "used" items at reduced price. It was sort of an ancient "next to new" shop.

And we thought the concept of a discount store was a modern idea!

Many Christians of that time were poor since they were out of favor with the powers that were in control. The shambles was the place for them to get the necessities of life at a price they could afford. That was good. Many Christians among them were confused by the practice of eating food that had been offered or sacrificed to idols. That was bad.

The question above was presented to Paul for his clarification. What he writes in 1 Corinthians 9 is practical advice to us today. The answer to the question is, "Yes, we do." However, what we do may have consequences to a weaker brother or sister.

Paul makes the case that the idol in reality is nothing. It is just a piece of wood, stone, or whatever. It has no power; it cannot speak or walk. It is not real. Therefore, eating meat that was sacrificed to it doesn't matter before the true God of Heaven.

However, there were still those for whom this issue was a problem. If you had purchased that meat and served it to them as your dinner guests, they would not have eaten it for conscience sake. They knew it had been consecrated to an offensive pagan god, so there is no way they would eat it.

In 1 Corinthians 8:8-13, Paul sums up the matter:

> But meat commendeth us not to God: for neither, if we eat, are we the better; neither, if we eat not, are we the worse. But take heed lest by any means this liberty of yours become a stumblingblock to them that are weak. For if any man see thee which hast knowledge sit at meat in the idol's temple, shall not the conscience of him which is weak be emboldened to eat those things which are offered to idols; And through thy knowledge shall the weak brother perish, for whom Christ died? But when ye sin so against the brethren, and wound their weak conscience, ye sin against Christ. Wherefore, if meat make my brother to offend, I will eat no flesh while the world standeth, lest I make my brother to offend.

It seems the issues of "social" drinking, attendance at movies, dances, smoking, and a whole host of other things are up for debate in every generation. The argument goes, "I know how to keep it under control," or " I have no problem with it." Oh, you think so? Maybe. Maybe not! However, when someone who may not be well grounded in their faith sees a person they view as a mentor or mature Christian come out of a bar, or have a glass of wine with dinner let's say, their whole life may take a turn for the worse as a result. They may think, "If it is okay for that person, it is okay for me." But it isn't.

There was a time not so many years ago, when, if a Christian went to a dance, a movie theater, a bar, or even a restaurant where alcoholic beverages were sold, it was considered worldly conduct. Most Christians would not go shopping on the Lord's Day. It was frowned upon by a Bible-believing church and the general congregation. Most of the Christian colleges of a generation ago had written policies that students had to sign—a pledge, if you will—that they would not be involved in certain things like those listed above, or they would face expulsion.

Today, some pastors have gone so far as to give their seal of approval for beer or a glass of wine with dinner. It is not uncommon for many believers to go to the movies. For that matter, now the movies that would never have been viewed by a conscientious Christian come to us via cable or rentals with no second thoughts about the profanity, nudity, or other forms of ungodly behavior. The level of confusion this creates in the eyes of a new believer is high, and if that is the case, what is the level of confusion created in the eyes of the unbeliever?

Paul's statement in verse 13 is a good rule for daily life: "Wherefore, if meat [or some other issue] make my brother to offend, I will eat no flesh while the world standeth, lest I make my brother to offend."

I Corinthians 10:3

And did all eat the same spiritual meat

For the sake of context, here are the first few verses of 1 Corinthians 10:

> Moreover, brethren, I would not that ye should be ignorant, how that all our fathers were under the cloud, and all passed through the sea; And were all baptized unto Moses in the cloud and in the sea; And did all eat the same spiritual meat; And did all drink the same spiritual drink: for they drank of that spiritual Rock that followed them: and that Rock was Christ. But with many of them God was not well pleased: for they were overthrown in the wilderness (vss. 1–5).

When the Children of Israel left Egypt, there must have been a level of excitement and anticipation unrivaled by almost all other events in history. Free at last! Everything is good!

Oops! Not so fast! "Who are those people following us in chariots?" The person first to see them and raise the alarm surely had a stab of fear go through to the core of his very being! The Egyptians, suddenly aware that they had just excused their slave labor force, and also suddenly aware that they would have to work instead of burden their slaves, realized they had made a grave mistake.

When Moses commanded them to follow him and step into the Red Sea, they surely thought he had gone mad, but when the waters opened, deliverance was before them. Figuratively, they were united as a people when they walked through the Red Sea on dry ground and were protected under the cloud of God's presence as they traveled. God gave them unexpected security and He provided for all of their needs. Their "spiritual meat" was more than the manna they found each day. They were being led by none other than the Lord Jesus Christ, Himself. His presence was with them every day.

When we read the account of their wanderings in the wilderness, we can easily point a wagging finger toward them and self-righteously think we would never make mistakes like they did. Really? We are just as guilty as they in our low level of faithfulness and trust toward the Lord. They were overthrown by their own lack of willingness to follow Him. We lose blessings when we do not do His will in our lives.

Nationally, we as a modern people are just as vulnerable as they to overthrow. We see our enemies trying to overthrow governments around the world. It would be foolish to think that they are all driven by pure thoughts. We have seen our faith-based society turn its back on God in our schools, in our governments, and even in many of our churches. We have turned to trusting in our own wisdom, goodness and abilities rather that believe that, "There is none righteous, no, not one" (Romans 3:10). Our reliance is on us, not Him. Because of that, our freedoms, our national identity and our very lives are in serious jeopardy.

When Israel trusted themselves and mingled their traditions and blood with the pagan societies around them, they paid dearly. The warning in 2 Corinthians 6:14 holds true in more than marriage relationships: "Be ye not unequally yoked together with unbelievers: for what fellowship hath righteousness with unrighteousness? and what communion hath light with darkness?"

As a nation, we have welcomed the "tired, poor, wretched masses yearning to breathe free" to our shores. In generations past, they gladly became "Americans" and mixed in with those already here, proudly working and serving beside us. As others have come more recently, many of them have not assimilated into our society. They have maintained their belief systems and traditions, refusing to blend in with American life, and have become a threat to our national existence with the help and encouragement of our government.

We will indeed all eat the same spiritual meat, but unless we are very careful, that meat may be spoiled and not safe to eat!

I Corinthians 16:14

Let all your things be done with charity

The apostle Paul is winding up his letter to the church in Corinth with these words: "Watch ye, stand fast in the faith, quit you like men, be strong. Let all your things be done with charity. I beseech you, brethren, (ye know the house of Stephanas, that it is the firstfruits of Achaia, and that they have addicted themselves to the ministry of the saints,) That ye submit yourselves unto such, and to every one that helpeth with us, and laboureth" (vss. 13–16).

That he starts out commanding us to be watchful, to be true to the faith, that we act like men and to be strong seems to be in contrast with being charitable. Reading on, Paul mentions his first converts in Achaia who went on to be totally dedicated to the point of addiction in serving the Lord on behalf of other believers. There is a connection. It takes great strength of character to faithfully and cheerfully serve others.

To submit to the will of another is difficult at best. When the one being submitted to is Christ, it is a bit easier, but it is still against our human nature. When we selflessly submit to the needs of others, it is a true sign of dedication to the Lord.

Let all your things be done with love. Can we be honest? Some people are rather hard to love. If you aren't sure about that, look in the mirror, and you will see the face of one who has tested at least one other person's patience and ability to love to the extreme. That is human nature, and unfortunately, human nature is something we can't escape.

If you have a godly pastor, you are fortunate. For him to be a tireless proclaimer of the Word of God, a soul-winner, a manager, cheerleader, shoulder to cry upon, prayer warrior, and all-around good guy is not the easiest job in the world. It is a calling. For him to do all of his duties as shepherd of the flock without love would be impossible.

This verse says, "Let all your things be done with charity." This is personal. All YOUR things . . . Our pastors often have a thankless job. They are not allowed to be human. They cannot make mistakes. They live in glass houses. Their children are under a microscope. They are allowed to forget nothing, and there are some other things they had better not remember! Most of all, they must always greet us with a smile, a cheerful tone, and be there any time we call. You betcha, the preacher does not have an easy job!

Is it any surprise that there are so few heeding God's call to the ministry today! We expect perfection, but as we read this passage, we realize Paul is talking about the leaders of a local flock. If they are godly men, we are expected to be in submission to their leadership as from God, meaning this verse comes back full circle: we need to show our charity, or love, just as much as we expect our pastor to show it toward us. A tall order, indeed.

II Corinthians 5:7

*For we walk by faith,
not by sight*

Some things are very difficult to remember in the heat of the battle. Everyday life has a way of making us walk more by sight than by faith. Our wisdom, we think, is sufficient; however, God may have a different way for us to go about our lives than the way we may want to go.

Reading the context of this verse (which is a good idea no matter what Scripture portions we read) shows the expansiveness of this verse. For the next minute, let's just take the verse by itself, as it is often quoted even by people in the world.

Most of us walk by sight. We do our everyday tasks without careful thought. When was the last time you thought carefully about tying your shoe? It is automatic for all of us fortunate enough to live without disabilities. We don't agonize over the route to take when we go to work since we know it blindfolded. We know the way around the house in the dark because we have navigated it in daylight enough to not think about it—or at least not until we trip over something left in the middle of the floor.

If you were a believer in Christ when you first started to drive a car, it is safe to assume you had a moment or more of serious prayer as you put the key in the ignition. That practice continued for an extended period of time. How about now? When, other than in the last snow or ice storm, was the last time you reminded the Lord that you knew He was your source of safety and you were relying on Him?

We don't show concern for the everyday issues in life when we pray. The big things like a marriage partner or new job? Of course. What to buy at the grocery store? Probably not. Which pair of shoes to buy? Maybe not. Which car, what house, what job, what doctor? Probably yes. What is the difference? It is either self confidence or lack of faith in the Lord's interest in even the small things in our lives.

If we walk by faith, even these smaller things should be things we take before the Lord. Fortunately, we don't need to ask the Lord when or how to take a breath since it is an automatic function in a healthy person. But wait, in Acts 17:24–25 "God that made the world and all things therein, seeing that he is Lord of heaven and earth, dwelleth not in temples made with hands; Neither is worshipped with men's hands, as though he needed any thing, seeing he giveth to all life, and breath, and all things. . . ."

Even our breath is a gift from Him. We don't know if we will get another, so each breath we take is by faith. How much more will we appreciate something if we don't take it for granted. Most of us get our eyes examined about once a year. Maybe a faith exam is in order, too!

II Corinthians 13:12

Greet one another with an holy kiss

Ah, yes. The favorite verse of young romantics everywhere.

Seriously, as Paul drew his second letter to the Corinthian church to a close, he no doubt was thinking of many of the people he knew there. They were people whom he had led to saving faith in the Lord, others he may have discipled, and the spiritual leaders with whom he had a special bond were never far from Paul's thinking. Each of his letters either lists people or has a similar greeting.

When one becomes a believer in Jesus Christ, he becomes a son (or daughter) of God. There is a familial bond that can't be explained in normal terms. As Romans 8:16–17 says, "The Spirit itself beareth witness with our spirit, that we are the children of God: And if children, then heirs; heirs of God, and joint-heirs with Christ; if so be that we suffer with him, that we may be also glorified together."

Just as you may have parents, a brother or sister, aunt or uncle, or a best friend from whom you are separated by the miles, you may send a card or letter and in your closing, add "X"s or "O"s representing kisses and hugs to remind them of your love for them, Paul did the same.

In many cultures, people will kiss each other on the cheeks. We see this among some of the Middle Eastern cultures. In Eastern Europe it is customary even for men to kiss men on the lips as a proper gesture of affection. Missionaries will often tell of being caught off guard and surprised by the practice. We will usually stop at a hand shake, maybe a hug if the person is someone we really care about or respect, but we stop short of a real kiss.

A holy kiss. It doesn't take much imagination to understand what an unholy kiss might be. A holy kiss might be harder to define. Suffice it to say, it is not a romantic gesture. It, or a proper hug, is a way to let someone know you care about them, that you respect them, and that you love them with a godly love. Within a church social structure, there may be any number of people who would fall into the realm of those we would care about as Paul is expressing his care.

Maybe the old song "They'll know we are Christians by our love" comes into play here. We can act warmly enough around business associates and friends in the world. How do we react to our brothers and sisters in Christ? Would a casual observer seeing our interaction with fellow believers get the idea that we loved our "family" in the Lord? We would hope so.

II Corinthians 13:13

All the saints salute you

In this verse, Paul is winding down his second letter to the Corinthian church. He has traveled the circuit between the various churches he had planted, doubtlessly carrying letters and verbal greetings from place to place. The level of warmth that surely had been built between the various locations was great. They knew they were a minority in a hostile political and religious environment. They knew persecution. They knew what it meant to be hated, but they also knew the embodiment of Truth as found in the person of Jesus Christ. They knew how He had changed their lives and how He could change the lives of any who would allow Him entrance.

The church in Corinth had its problems. They are clearly laid out in the two epistles we have, yet it would appear that these problems had been set straight. Paul didn't say, "All the saints condemn you," or "All the churches know about your problems and are praying for you to get your act together."

"All the saints salute you." All the saints hold you in high regard. You are being prayed for and respected.

Here in a simple verse, we have a guide for us today. Even with Facebook, cell phones, Internet, and websites, we seem to feel there is a competition to see which individual church wins some prize or accolade. Our fight is against the devil and all of the evil around us, not against other Bible-believing churches.

It has often been said that we may be surprised when we see who is in Heaven living in the mansion next to ours. They just might be from a church we would never have dreamed of working with in this life on planet Earth.

Most people who can relate the events unfolding in our news with end-times prophecy have a sense of anticipation. We know it will not be long before we see the Lord face to face. On that day we will have set all of our differences aside. What could be accomplished if we could set even a few of them aside and work with other true believers today to win souls for Christ before it is eternally too late?

Oh, Lord Jesus, on that day, all the saints will salute you! Revelation 4 portrays the scene when, after the Rapture, we will stand before the throne of God and crowns will be cast at the feet of the One Who purchased our salvation with His own precious blood. Here is part of that chapter:

> After this I looked, and, behold, a door was opened in heaven: and the first voice which I heard was as it were of a trumpet talking with me; which said, Come up hither, and I will show thee things which must be hereafter. And immediately I was in the spirit; and, behold, a throne was set in heaven, and one sat on the throne. . . . And the four beasts had each of them six wings about him; and they were full of eyes within: and they rest not day and night, saying, Holy, holy, holy, Lord God Almighty, which was, and is, and is to come. And when those beasts give glory and honour and thanks to him that sat on the throne, who liveth for ever and ever, The four and twenty elders fall down before him that sat on the throne, and worship him that liveth for ever and ever, and cast their crowns before the throne, saying, Thou art worthy, O Lord, to receive glory and honour and power: for thou hast created all things, and for thy pleasure they are and were created.

Lord Jesus, on that day, we will indeed salute you as we bow before you in thanks, humility, love, and awe. The One Who alone is worthy will be crowned and receive the glory, honor and power that is rightfully His as the King of the universe.

Galatians 5:9

A little leaven leaveneth the whole lump

We have taken this biblical phrase to the common vernacular of, A little goes a long way! At the time of this writing, we from the American northeast look back on a few seasons of more snow and rain than most of us would prefer. For a skier, a lot of snow is a benefit. For most of the rest of us, it was more than enough. Truth be told, we would appreciate a little more "global warming" in our winters.

Leaven is yeast. A little in a lump of dough makes the bread rise, but too much makes a mess! Every once and a while, someone has handed us a container and, with a smile, says: "This is the starter for friendship bread. Enjoy it and share some with friends. . . ." It would seem there is a commonality between friendship bread and the situation in which Mickey Mouse found himself in the Disney classic film *The Sorcerer's Apprentice.* Like those brooms with the buckets of water, the friendship bread is a gift that keeps on giving. And giving. And . . .

Too much of a good thing is always too much. However, not enough can be an equal problem. Parenting is a tightrope act between being too permissive and too restrictive. Management practice in business is similar. In every area of endeavor, we can see extremes that would result in problems. In our dealings with others, we need to know where to draw the line, when to back off, and when to press on. Wisdom comes from the Lord as we are clearly taught in the Proverbs.

In Galatians 5:1, Paul instructs us to "Stand fast therefore in the liberty wherewith Christ hath made us free, and be not entangled again with the yoke of bondage."

In our walk with the Lord, there can never be too close of a relationship. In our every day lives, however, our liberty in Christ must be tempered with restraint. Since leaven is also compared to sin, this verse also reminds us that even those things we think of as "little" sins are still a big thing to God. A seemingly small act can cast long shadows that will never go away.

Ephesians 4:5

One Lord, one faith, one baptism

It doesn't take long until one hears this verse used as a club over one's head to conform to a standard set by someone who considers himself to be "right." While we have one Lord, while the Bible teaches one true faith, and while there is just one baptism by which we are identified as members of the Body of Christ, namely, through His shed blood, this verse is not a catch-all to force us into fellowship with people who have clearly unbiblical practices or openly heretical doctrines mixed in with some elements of truth.

Unfortunately, through the time since our Lord walked on earth, and especially at this current time in history, the Lord Jesus Christ is not acknowledged to be the Lord of all by all men. That day is still future when all will confess the Lord Christ. "For it is written, As I live, saith the Lord, every knee shall bow to me, and every tongue shall confess to God. So then every one of us shall give account of himself to God. Let us not therefore judge one another any more: but judge this rather, that no man put a stumblingblock or an occasion to fall in his brother's way" (Romans 14:11–13).

The command of Paul is for us to be sure we are in a right relationship with the Lord and then with our fellow man, so as not to cause someone else to be hindered in their spiritual growth. Schism frequently comes when we do not recognize the authority of the Lord and His Word in our lives. Churches split and new denominations form more because human beings think that faith and baptism are defined by man-made standards than by the Word of God.

The number of denominations and sects within "Christendom" are too many to list. When the Lord comes back to rule and reign on the earth, and then through eternity, there will be no second thought of whose standard is the rule. He will be in charge. There will be endless divisions until then. Surely His return will be a blessing in many ways we do not even imagine at this time. Unity among believers will be a wonderful and refreshing change.

Ephesians 4:27

Neither give place to the devil

This verse appears within a rather long portion that cannot be ignored: Ephesians 4:21–5:2:

> If so be that ye have heard him, and have been taught by him, as the truth is in Jesus: That ye put off concerning the former conversation the old man, which is corrupt according to the deceitful lusts; And be renewed in the spirit of your mind; And that ye put on the new man, which after God is created in righteousness and true holiness. Wherefore putting away lying, speak every man truth with his neighbour: for we are members one of another. Be ye angry, and sin not: let not the sun go down upon your wrath: Neither give place to the devil. Let him that stole steal no more: but rather let him labour, working with his hands the thing which is good, that he may have to give to him that needeth. Let no corrupt communication proceed out of your mouth, but that which is good to the use of edifying, that it may minister grace unto the hearers. And grieve not the holy Spirit of God, whereby ye are sealed unto the day of redemption. Let all bitterness, and wrath, and anger, and clamour, and evil speaking, be put away from you, with all malice: And be ye kind one to another, tenderhearted, forgiving one another, even as God for Christ's sake hath forgiven you. Be ye therefore followers of God, as dear children; And walk in love, as Christ also hath loved us, and hath given himself for us. . . .

If we had no context whatsoever, this verse would still be important.

Whenever we allow the devil to have opportunity in our lives, we lose and other people may also be harmed, but most of all, the matchless name of our Lord Jesus Christ suffers. Whenever Satan gets his foot in the door, the results are that a Christian testimony is damaged.

In our family relationships, the verse prior tells us to not let the sun go down without our anger or strained relationships being set straight. How many marriages have been ruined because something went wrong, wasn't gotten right, and grew to be larger-than-life as the days went on. How many children and parents are estranged because someone wasn't willing to say, "I'm sorry," or "It was my fault."

In our relationship with the Lord, pride or self-will can easily get in the way, and before we know it, we have become estranged with Him. Great blessings are missed, and eternal rewards are lost.

When we learn to forgive others "even as God for Christ's sake hath forgiven you," we learn one of the greatest lessons in life. It may take a whole lifetime to learn it, but if we do actually learn it, we have taken a major step forward in our spiritual lives.

James 4:10 instructs: "Humble yourselves in the sight of the Lord, and he shall lift you up." And 1 Peter 5:5–6 admonishes us to "be clothed with humility: for God resisteth the proud, and giveth grace to the humble. Humble yourselves therefore under the mighty hand of God, that he may exalt you in due time."

Both passages offer the key for success with others in relationship with us or with those in authority over us. If we are willing to take the attitude of humility rather than pride or stubbornness, God will bring the circumstances around to His glory and our gain. What a wonderful thing when a simple expression of humility brings about a complete change in the reaction of someone with whom we could just as well have been in battle. How our homes and lives could improve if we did not allow Satan to get the upper hand. First John 4:4 is good news: ". . . greater is he that is in you, than he that is in the world." That "greater" One in us will surely give us the grace to maintain a right relationship with others.

In John 16:33, Jesus gives the words of great comfort: "These things I have spoken unto you, that in me ye might have peace. In the world ye shall have tribulation: but be of good cheer; I have overcome the world."

Be not ye therefore partakers with them

Be ye therefore followers of God, as dear children; And walk in love, as Christ also hath loved us, and hath given himself for us an offering and a sacrifice to God for a sweetsmelling savour. But fornication, and all uncleanness, or covetousness, let it not be once named among you, as becometh saints; Neither filthiness, nor foolish talking, nor jesting, which are not convenient: but rather giving of thanks. For this ye know, that no whoremonger, nor unclean person, nor covetous man, who is an idolater, hath any inheritance in the kingdom of Christ and of God. Let no man deceive you with vain words: for because of these things cometh the wrath of God upon the children of disobedience. Be not ye therefore partakers with them. For ye were sometimes darkness, but now are ye light in the Lord: walk as children of light.

—Ephesians 5:1–8

There is a line drawn here. On one side, we are admonished to be followers of God. On the other, we are commanded to not be involved with the things of the world.

This thin line does not separate us from everyday necessary things. We are not told to become hermits in an isolated cave. We still have to work at our job, we have to deal with our families, we need to be involved in the community, church, PTA, whatever else. All of these are fine and have a proper place, but the list in the verses above separates the everyday ordinary things from those that are sinful and unworthy of our time and effort.

Verse 8 reminds us that we were not born righteous, but were submerged in the darkness of sin. Now, because of what Jesus did for us on the cross, we are expected to avoid those things that would drag us back into the world and sinful living and walk in the light as children of the One Who is the Light of the World.

The Apostle Peter said it this way in 1 Peter 2:7–11:

Unto you therefore which believe he is precious: but unto them which be disobedient, the stone which the builders disallowed, the same is made the head of the corner, And a stone of stumbling, and a rock of offence, even to them which stumble at the word, being disobedient: whereunto also they were appointed. But ye are a chosen generation, a royal priesthood, an holy nation, a peculiar people; that ye should show forth the praises of him who hath called you out of darkness into his marvellous light: Which in time past were not a people, but are now the people of God: which had not obtained mercy, but now have obtained mercy. Dearly beloved, I beseech you as strangers and pilgrims, abstain from fleshly lusts, which war against the soul. . . .

Colossians 2:21

Touch not; taste not; handle not

The more things change, the more they remain the same. In less than fifty years after our Lord ascended back into Heaven, people were worshipping angels, spouting off as though they knew things that they couldn't possibly know, and so much more. They had strayed far from true worship and, just as a part that is not attached to its body, were not being spiritually nourished. They were set up for the fall under the guidance of false teachers.

Without context, this verse sounds like a warning to someone who is diabetic while in a snack shop full of sugary treats. Obviously, it isn't.

Looking at the surrounding verses gives a clearer view of what Paul is trying to say.

> Let no man beguile you of your reward in a voluntary humility and worshipping of angels, intruding into those things which he hath not seen, vainly puffed up by his fleshly mind, And not holding the Head, from which all the body by joints and bands having nourishment ministered, and knit together, increaseth with the increase of God. Wherefore if ye be dead with Christ from the rudiments of the world, why, as though living in the world, are ye subject to ordinances, (Touch not; taste not; handle not; Which all are to perish with the using;) after the commandments and doctrines of men? Which things have indeed a show of wisdom in will worship, and humility, and neglecting of the body; not in any honour to the satisfying of the flesh. If ye then be risen with Christ, seek those things which are above,

where Christ sitteth on the right hand of God. Set your affection on things above, not on things on the earth. For ye are dead, and your life is hid with Christ in God.

—Colossians 2:18–3:3

Our worship needs to be focused not on men, not on ourselves—whether being puffed up as though we are important, or in false humility—but on the Lord, the One Who purchased our salvation and is now in Heaven preparing our future eternal home.

Our eternal rewards for service are in jeopardy. We can work hard, thinking we are serving Him, only to find our accomplishments burned in the fire of testing. "If any man's work abide which he hath built thereupon, he shall receive a reward. If any man's work shall be burned, he shall suffer loss: but he himself shall be saved; yet so as by fire" (1 Corinthians 3:14–15).

It doesn't matter what areas of interest may occupy our earthly lives since we all have to make a living and meet the needs of our families, homes, and communities, but we err if these things become our primary focus. It is difficult to remember that our temporal life is short compared with eternity, so a legitimate question is, do we take the time we should in prayer, Bible reading, witnessing, and seeking those things which are above? We who are born again through the precious blood of the Lord Jesus Christ will spend eternity in Heaven where our affections and interests should be focused even now.

We can't leave this passage without a comment regarding the worship of angels. An angel is a ministering spirit and is either dedicated to the service of God or, in the case of the angels who fell from grace, dedicated to the service of Satan.

There is a considerable amount of attention being devoted to angels in our time. Many people pray to them asking for their help in daily tasks, venerate them, and depict them as though they were our servants, not the Lord's. So-called Christian stores are full of angel plaques, pictures, and statuettes. The Internet is full of cute poems and "forwards" that indicate an angel was behind the message we may have just received from a well meaning friend. Oh, and they almost have the warning that, if you don't send the message or poem to seven people within the next seven minutes, you will miss a blessing.

Satan must be laughing up his sleeve. Whenever he has been successful in diverting our attention from the Lord to something or someone else, he is happy. His demonic angels are very active trying to keep our focus away from God, but Satan's angels are losers! They got the boot from God when they sided with Satan. Needless to say, they are not interested in leading our thoughts to the eternal creator God. Our prayers are to be addressed to the Lord, not angels, saints, or anyone else venerated whose name is not Jesus Christ, the Lord. As John put it in 1 John 5:13–15: "These things have I written unto you that believe on the name of the Son of God; that ye may know that ye have eternal life, and that ye may believe on the name of the Son of God. And this is the confidence that we have in him, that, if we ask any thing according to his will, he heareth us: And if we know that he hear us, whatsoever we ask, we know that we have the petitions that we desired of him."

Rejoice evermore

We have several verses that follow in rapid succession that fit our "One Liners" definition.

The first of these verses is not translated from the original language saying, "When you are feeling good, and when you want to, rejoice." It dogmatically states: "Rejoice evermore." A narrow constraint is presented here. We are not asked; it is not suggested. It is commanded.

But I don't feel like it!

Too bad. Get over it. A person led by his feelings usually goes down a hard path through life. Feelings are fickle. They are often satanically controlled, as well.

But you don't understand my circumstances.

That is true; I do not. Get over them. The person who is under his circumstances is seldom enjoying anything but feeling sorry for himself. Don't ask that person "How are you doing?" You will regret it! She will give "organ recitals" of her latest operations. He isn't happy unless he isn't happy about something. The person who is "under the circumstances" is not overcoming as Christ would have His children to do.

What a way to live. If you want to call that living.

The Apostle John wrote in 1 John 2:12–14:

I write unto you, little children, because your sins are forgiven you for his name's sake. I write unto you, fathers, because ye have known him that is from the beginning. I write unto you, young men, because ye have overcome the wicked one. I write unto you, little children, because ye have known the Father. I have written unto you, fathers, because ye have known him that is from the beginning. I have written unto you, young men, because ye are strong, and the word of God abideth in you, and ye have overcome the wicked one.

What a difference it makes to realize we are already victorious over the devil!

Fanny Crosby was blind, but she was not a complainer. She had a relationship with the Lord during her long life that resulted in some of the most loved pages in our hymnbooks. Her poems, set to music by others, have been a great blessing to any who have sung or heard them. Though blind, her poems were full of "sight" and insight as she longed to see the face of her Savior.

More recently, the testimony of John Bishop from Rosebud, Arkansas, stands out. Through illness, he lost all memory. All of it. He had to "start at the very beginning" with A-B-C and Do-Re-Mi. At the time of this writing, despite the fact that he is blind and physically in constant pain, his testimony and smile are difficult to imagine. He radiates Christ and His love.

A young man from Philadelphia, while attending college studying to be a preacher of the gospel, was led to pray one night that he knew that everything he had, his home, car, bank account, and his health were gifts from God and was giving them back to Him to be used as He saw fit.

Matt Guzzi found out soon after that he had an unusual kind of cancer that had no cure. His life was not a long one, but he used the days he had to faithfully proclaim Christ to all who would hear. Video recordings of his testimony and vision to serve the Lord have reached more since his passing to glory than he may have had opportunity to reach had he lived a normal life.

Mark 8:36–37 records the words of Christ: "Whosoever will come after me, let him deny himself, and take up his cross, and follow me. For whosoever will save his life shall lose it; but whosoever shall lose his life for my sake and the gospel's, the same shall save it. For what shall it profit a man, if he shall gain the whole world, and lose his own soul? Or what shall a man give in exchange for his soul?"

Fanny, John, and Matt made decisions to rejoice in the Lord, not wallow in their problems. Why did the Lord allow them such hard lives? Maybe you will want to ask Him when you get to Heaven if you need to. It will be clear when we get there that they were able to influence more people and lead more people to saving faith in the Lord because of their problems than if they had lived normal lives. Somewhere in the course of their lives, they made the decision that whether by life or by death, they wanted Christ to be the One Who received the glory.

First Thessalonians 5:18 is in the middle of this run of "One Liners," but even though it is too long to be one, let's include it here: "In every thing give thanks: for this is the will of God in Christ Jesus concerning you."

Rejoice today, rejoice tomorrow, the next day, and every day. Establish the habit now and you WILL rejoice evermore in the presence of the Lord!

1 Thessalonians 5:17

Pray without ceasing

Prayer is work. When Christ prayed to His Father in the Garden of Gethsemane just before His crucifixion, we are told that, "And being in an agony he prayed more earnestly: and his sweat was as it were great drops of blood falling down to the ground" (Luke 22:44).

"Sweet Hour of Prayer" is a great song, but the reality is that most of us would be tongue-tied in ten minutes, twenty at the most, if there were big things happening in our lives, but an hour?

Pray without ceasing? No, it does not mean that is all we should do day in and day out, every moment of every day. It refers to an attitude of prayer. The connection is made, and you can visualize that the Lord is on the other end just waiting for us to pick up the phone on our end. As Hebrews 7:25 says, He is ever living to make intercession for us. He is there at a moment's notice.

We can ask the Lord to guide us as we go through the day, we can breathe a "Thank You" at any time, or even a "Wow, Lord, thanks! That was great!" When we hear an ambulance or fire siren, we could offer a simple prayer for those in need or for protection for those who serve us as fire and police personnel, and our military overseas. Anything.

We would chatter to a companion about everything that comes to mind, so why not "keep the phone off the hook" and talk to the Lord the same way. He is real! He really does want to hear from us about the things that are part of our lives. He loves us and wants our fellowship.

1 Thessalonians 5:19

Quench not the Spirit

It may be safe to say that most of us do not comprehend what this verse means. We know how to quench a thirst and to drench a fire, but what does this verse mean?

Often people say that someone quenched the Spirit of God by "throwing cold water" on a ministry, on a struggling believer, or some other effort to glorify God.

Consider: To quench a thirst would be to satisfy it. If one is dry and parched from a trek across the Mojave Desert, all he wants is water. Lots of water. Maybe even a little more than that. After a while, that person's thirst would be satisfied or quenched.

Surely, the standard teaching of not quenching or hindering the Spirit of God is true. One can easily thwart the ministry of the Spirit by getting in the way of those who are serving, or by making discouraging remarks, being a nay-sayer, or just by being a wet blanket working against those who are earnestly working for the Lord.

Here's a thought: Could this verse also have the concept that the Spirit of God should never be satisfied that we have done enough? If our attitude is that we can never do enough for the Kingdom of God; that we can always do something more as long as we have the strength to breathe, we will never need to worry that we have fulfilled the task before us.

This is not to say that nothing we do is ever good enough, but simply that, compared to One Who died in our place and gave His all to meet demands of the law that we never could meet on our own, our job is not complete until we have drawn our last breath. To give up before that time is to quench the Spirit's ability to use us for God's glory.

1 Thessalonians 5:20

Despise not prophesyings

"I prophesy the world will come to an end on _____." He offers a specific date.

Whenever you hear a self-proclaimed "prophet" say something like that, grab your wallet and your running shoes. A popular radio teacher has spent considerable time since the 1990s confusing people and persuading them to believe his heretical teaching. Who knows how many books he has sold, but worse, how many people have been disillusioned when his predictions did not come true, blaming God for not being faithful rather than blaming the false teacher. Human nature precludes that we will not blame ourselves for being snookered when we swallow the snake oil.

Based on this verse, should we accept this kind of teacher as valid? NO! This verse is not teaching us to accept the rantings of would-be fortune tellers, card readers, and sideshow barkers as valid.

Clearly, God's Word is warning us here to not despise those who faithfully and clearly teach and preach the Word of God. Watch out for those who will try to take a portion of Scripture and cram it into a mold that fits their desires rather than what the Scripture says. There have been many of those kind of teachers in the past. Indeed grab your wallet. They WILL pass the Colonel Sanders fried chicken collection bucket and expect you to fill it. They might even pass it twice! Keep those running shoes handy, too, since the more distance you can put between you and them, the better.

When a faithful preacher clearly expounds the Word and it steps on our toes, we had best pay attention and adjust our lives to match God's will for our lives. Don't ignore, don't discount, don't fail to pay attention to the clear teaching of the Word of God!

The Bereans were commended in Acts 18:11 because they carefully compared Scripture with Scripture. They didn't take a preacher's word for truth unless they knew it WAS truth. Many radio preachers and itinerant tent preachers have been true to the Word of God. They don't last long otherwise, but until the true colors of a false teacher are known, they can easily "shear" the sheep and cause considerable trouble in the flock. The more we know God's Word, the less likely we will be led astray by false teachers and preachers.

I Thessalonians 5:22

Abstain from all appearance of evil

"I have liberty in Christ. I can do anything that is not obvious sin. I know the difference between what is right and what is wrong. I have enough sense to make good choices. If you can't do what I can with a clear conscience, that is your problem, so don't you dare judge me."

Oh, we may never say that out loud, but it is easy to think that way. The result: we think we can go places and cause no harm to the weaker brother. The Christian, young in the faith, sees you go to a tap room and thinks, "If he can do it, I guess it is okay." In no time, that young believer is on the skids, having fallen to temptations that were too strong for his weak faith.

Even preachers who led national ministries found it was harder than they thought to keep from falling and they crashed and burned in disgrace when they got too close to the temptations of the world.

Witness to the lost, but do not join them in their sin. Keep your distance. For sure, run into a burning building to drag someone to safety, but don't sit there while the building burns around you and be involved in their folly. Christ is our example. Those who opposed Him tried to paste labels on Him. They called Him every name imaginable, going so far as to say He did miracles by the power of Satan. No one, however, was ever able to make any claim stick since His life was pure and His ministry true.

He rescued people from their sin but never got involved in those sins. There was a clear line drawn between those controlled by demons, and the Lord who cast the demons out of people. He didn't involve Himself in adultery even though He freed and forgave people who were bound in its grip.

When we walk our walk, and talk our talk, one of our greatest needs is to be careful to not allow for even the suggestion that our activities compromise our lives and testimony.

1 Thessalonians 5:25

Brethren, pray for us

Paul knew his personal ministry was being carried out in weak flesh. In various writings he mentioned several things that were physical limitations. He seems to have had bad eyes, he had been shipwrecked, and he had been beaten by the Roman authorities more than once. Most likely, some of his problems in later life were related to those beatings. Paul knew he could only serve the Lord as he was upheld in prayer by other believers.

We often hear mention of "prayer partners," or "prayer warriors." People who faithfully bring their list of friends, family, pastors, missionaries and others before the Lord are indeed the frontline warriors in the spiritual battle that rages around us.

If you have been in a Bible-believing church for any period of time, surely you have heard stories of unusual circumstances when something happened that could only be described as a miracle. The auto accident that would have been disastrous but was avoided by a hair's breadth; the missionary family that was threatened by hostile natives of a pagan culture, but the danger passed without incident or explanation; the serious illness that was cured, leaving doctors with no ability to comprehend. Sometimes we hear at a later time of one who was on their knees fervently lifting up the names of those involved before the throne of grace.

Second Kings 6:15–17 tells what happened when Gehazi learned a great lesson about God's protection of His own:

And when the servant of the man of God was risen early, and gone forth, behold, an host compassed the city both with horses and chariots. And his servant said unto him, Alas, my master! how shall we do? And he answered, Fear not: for they that be with us are more than they that be with them. And Elisha prayed, and said, LORD, I pray thee, open his eyes, that he may see. And the LORD opened the eyes of the young man; and he saw: and, behold, the mountain was full of horses and chariots of fire round about Elisha.

The world that day saw two men in the crosshairs of the Syrian army's wrath. Elisha saw the chariots of fire and the host of the Lord that was there to protect them.

Whether it is the Syrians, the Philistines, the Babylonians of old, or whatever member of the Foe-of-the-Believer club we may face, Ephesians 6:12–13 brings our ultimate enemy into focus as well as our defense: "For we wrestle not against flesh and blood, but against principalities, against powers, against the rulers of the darkness of this world, against spiritual wickedness in high places. Wherefore take unto you the whole armour of God, that ye may be able to withstand in the evil day, and having done all, to stand."

Paul knew, and we need to know, who our enemy is and that we are only as strong as the strength of the Lord when faith is exercised in our lives. He asked people everywhere to keep him in their prayers so that the Lord would be magnified and glorified in his life and ministry.

What then? notwithstanding, every way, whether in pretence, or in truth, Christ is preached; and I therein do rejoice, yea, and will rejoice. For I know that this shall turn to my salvation through your prayer, and the supply of the Spirit of Jesus Christ, According to my earnest expectation and my hope, that in nothing I shall be ashamed, but that with all boldness, as always, so now also Christ shall be magnified in my body, whether it be by life, or by death. For to me to live is Christ, and to die is gain.

—Philipians 1:18–21

Remember to pray for each other. Praying always with all prayer and supplication in the Spirit, and watching thereunto with all perseverance and supplication for all saints (Ephesians 6:18).

Never forget: our strength is not in ourselves, but in the Lord, and in the power of his might (Ephesians 6:10).

Greet all the brethren with an holy kiss

We already looked at 2 Corinthians 13:12. It is similar enough to say, turn back a few pages and see that earlier reference.

1 Timothy 4:11

These things command and teach

What things? The obvious broad answer is everything in God's Word. Let's narrow that down a little. In just this fourth chapter, Paul includes several major things we might consider. "Now the Spirit speaketh expressly, that in the latter times some shall depart from the faith, giving heed to seducing spirits, and doctrines of devils; Speaking lies in hypocrisy; having their conscience seared with a hot iron . . ." (4:1-3).

If we need another proof that these are the last days, here are some of the indicators: teachers who have become apostate, seducing spirits, doctrines of devils, and lying hypocrisy. We are warned often in Scripture of last-days deceptions. All around us we see those who are seductive with their false teaching. They attempt to make us feel good with the flowery words we want to hear, even if they are not true. Doctrines of devils surround us and are well illustrated in the world today by the *kaffiyia* of the militant Muslim.

Verse 6 is good teaching for the one who would serve the Lord in ministry. "If thou put the brethren in remembrance of these things, thou shalt be a good minister of Jesus Christ, nourished up in the words of faith and of good doctrine, whereunto thou hast attained."

While verse 8 includes the mantra for the lazy, "For bodily exercise profiteth little . . ." the rest of the verse is our best instruction for living a life that counts for the Lord: ". . . but godliness is profitable unto all things, having promise of the life that now is, and of that which is to come."

Our modern secular society certainly does not despise youth. Instead, it venerates it so that one would think the older we get, the less wise we are. The point in verse 12 seems to be that we are to follow Proverbs 22:6 while our children are young: "Train up a child in the way he should go: and when he is old, he will not depart from it." The result follows in the second half of verse 12, in that even a young person can be a good example of what a Christian should be.

Our role as parents is well spelled out. The TV, music, movies, Facebook, and Internet access of today will do nothing to encourage a young person to be an example of the believers, in word, in conversation, in charity, in spirit, in faith, in purity. It takes almost no time to realize their negative influence on the upcoming generation—if we are alert. Unfortunately, most of today's parents are not alert: they are inert.

"Tiger moms" have been in the news, generating no little bit of controversy. Parents who take their responsibility seriously know that the world is full of garbage. There is no difference in our responsibility to keep things off the floor that could harm a baby who has just discovered crawling, and keeping things away from the developing adolescent whose values are being shaped by either the society around him or by godly parents and church leaders. "Now, Johnny, don't touch the hot stove" may not be enough for all children. Sometimes a good smack on the hand, though it may produce a crocodile tear or two, is much better than the trip to the hospital with third degree burns.

The verse says to do more than teach. It requires us to lovingly command and teach. Be relentless. Persist. Take no prisoners. Expect results that will make a difference for eternity.

2 Timothy 4:12

And Tychicus have I sent to Ephesus

I knew in advance that there would be at least one like this . . . Thankfully, there is more to Tychicus than this single verse. Much more.

Paul is nearing the end of his life. He is an old man who has suffered much and accomplished more. He started out a zealot for Judiasm and ended a martyr for Jesus Christ. In his years he has appeared before the common man and the highest rulers of the land to present his testimony of faith in Jesus Christ. Now his travels have taken him to Rome where ultimately he will be beheaded for his faith. Rather than being fearful of, or angry about, what will follow, listen to his words in chapter 4:6–8: "For I am now ready to be offered, and the time of my departure is at hand. I have fought a good fight, I have finished my course, I have kept the faith: Henceforth there is laid up for me a crown of righteousness, which the Lord, the righteous judge, shall give me at that day: and not to me only, but unto all them also that love his appearing."

This is a personal letter, and in reality, we are reading someone else's mail, but the Holy Spirit inspired this as well as other keystone passages. Maybe we can hear some sadness as well as the sigh of a weary man, but it is primarily a victor's declaration. Here Paul mentions several people who were important in his life and for whom he had special messages.

Perhaps we can hear a bit of the disappointment he has in people he thought were dependable, or who would stay by his side in ministry.

"For Demas hath forsaken me, having loved this present world, and is departed unto Thessalonica; Crescens to Galatia, Titus unto Dalmatia" (Vs. 10).

While we know nothing more of Crescens, we do know that Titus was a faithful fellow-laborer with Paul and at this time had left Paul to minister elsewhere. While Paul surely rejoiced in Titus' ministry opportunity, it is clear that Paul missed his fellowship and encouragement.

There were those who were faithful, too: Verse 11 reveals the writer of one of the Gospels and the Book of the Acts of the Apostles: "Only Luke is with me." Then he wrote, "Take Mark, and bring him with thee: for he is profitable to me for the ministry." Mark was rejected in earlier writing as being unprofitable. It is an encouragement for any of us who may have failed along the way in our lives. Here we see that he got things right with both Paul and the Lord and was now profitable to Paul's ministry.

Ah, yes: "And Tychicus have I sent to Ephesus." In Acts 20 we see him first as one who traveled with Paul. In Ephesians 6 we learn he was trusted and beloved by Paul as one who ministered with him.

Paul's epistles contain a veritable "Who's Who," mentioning people who are being praised, thanked, or put in their place for what they did with, for, or against Paul. Tychicus is listed five times in Scripture. Once in Luke's account in Acts, the other four times by Paul, each time indicating he was a faithful fellowlaborer or messenger.

If Paul was so appreciative of him, think of the reward that may be his for his service to Paul but primarily to the Lord. We can be assured that what we do for Christ will indeed be rewarded. We do not have our names written in the pages of Bible, but the One Who wrote it has another book where our name is recorded. In Philippians 4:3, Paul writes: "And I entreat thee also, true yokefellow, help those women which laboured with me in the gospel, with Clement also, and with other my fellowlabourers, whose names are in the book of life."

Hebrews 6:3

And this will we do,
if God permit

Surely you have heard someone say something like, "I will do something, Lord willing, and the creeks don't rise," as a colloquial way of saying they plan to do something as long as the Lord gives strength and another day in which to do it.

So often we make plans for later in the day, next week, next year, and far into the future with no thought of God's will for our lives. We plow ahead as if we were truly the master of our destiny and fate. To some degree, man needs to expect life to go on as normal because it does to a reasonable degree. One can't plan for the accidents, health crises, natural disasters, and incongruities of life. Most people didn't expect the events of September 11, 2001. President John F. Kennedy didn't expect that sunny day in Dallas to be his last day breathing on earth. The thousands who lost their lives in northern Japan in March 2011 never expected the earthquake, let alone the tsunami that followed it. We could add to the list many more surprises that interrupt everyday life.

For many of us, God did not permit something but intervened by direct or indirect means to prevent it. The best laid plans of men are often brought to naught. We can be thankful in many cases that He did not allow us to do something that would have proven to be a disaster. Even when we think God made a mistake, He didn't.

How easy it is for us to go on our merry way thinking our plans are all rubber stamped by God, forgetting that in prayer we should have submitted them to Him first for approval.

James 1:16

Do not err, my beloved brethren

That sounds like very good advice. Don't make a mistake. Mistakes can be dangerous!

"I thought it said take three every hour, not one every three hours."

"Oh, was that a red light?"

"Did I forget to add those extra three zeros to the check?"

"My appointment is tomorrow, isn't it?"

"I don't need your God in my life. I am doing fine by myself, thank you!"

Again, a little context would be helpful: "But every man is tempted, when he is drawn away of his own lust, and enticed. Then when lust hath conceived, it bringeth forth sin: and sin, when it is finished, bringeth forth death. Do not err, my beloved brethren" (vss. 14-16).

God does not tempt us to do evil. That would make Him no different than the devil. He allows us to be tried, if for no other reason than to allow us to see how far we would go if we did not have Him holding on to our leash. It can be good for us occasionally to see how weak we really are and what human nature really is.

When temptation comes, what we do with it is the test of what we really are. Temptation is not sin. Yielding to it is. It is our lust or selfish desire that takes us down the path of sin. No matter what type of sin may be involved, if carried far enough, it will bring sorrow, pain and ultimately death. For the unsaved person, eternal death—separation from

God for all eternity in the never quenched fires of Hell.

Don't make the worst mistake of all: neglecting to confess your sin to the God Who alone has paid the price for it so you can experience forgiveness, Heaven and His presence for eternity.

1 John 4:19

We love him,
because he first loved us

Love at first sight! Ah, isn't it wonderful!

Remember when you were a teenager and he or she walked by and the whole world stopped on its axis: birds started singing, rainbows were everywhere, the air was filled with a sweet perfume. You were in love!

Maybe it was like that, maybe not. Most of us can look back at seeing someone that we thought was God's gift to us. Sometimes that works out; often it doesn't. Usually it is a process of winning the affection of the object of our attention. A smile, note, flowers, cookies, a friendly word again and again until that person actually realizes you exist.

Before we come to faith in Christ, we usually don't see how much He is showering His love upon us. He has been there all along, showing us how much He loves us in many ways, both subtle and obvious. When He finally gets our attention, we realize He has shown His love to us in countless ways for a long time.

Once we realize the depth of love He has for us, our only response can be for us to love Him in return. Fortunately, we will have all eternity to make up for being slow in comprehending His love.

And I will give him the morning star

The verses leading up to verse 28 help us to understand it. "But that which ye have already hold fast till I come. And he that overcometh, and keepeth my works unto the end, to him will I give power over the nations: And he shall rule them with a rod of iron; as the vessels of a potter shall they be broken to shivers: even as I received of my Father. And I will give him the morning star" (vss. 25–28).

The church of Thyatira had much for which to be commended, but, there was one area where they had compromised. They cooperated with the apostate religious system of their day. Oil trying to mix with water. God was not about to forget that and would judge those who had been unfaithful. Those who had been faithful, however, were not going to be condemned with those who deserved it.

Hold fast to the truth. Jesus is coming again. Soon! The churches around us are not holding true, so we who understand the problem must. Those who have forsaken the truth will be judged severely, but those who have remained true will receive the morning star.

Jesus Christ is the bright and morning star.

If any man have an ear, let him hear

This sentence or others that are very similar appear more than a dozen times in the New Testament. Whenever Christ is speaking, and when He repeats Himself that many times, it would be a good idea for us to pay attention.

This is the last time the phrase appears in Scripture, and the only time it stands alone as a verse unto itself. It is almost as if the Word of God is adding an exclamation point to it to draw our attention to it.

Since "All scripture is given by inspiration of God, and is profitable for doctrine, for reproof, for correction, for instruction in righteousness: That the man of God may be perfect, throughly furnished unto all good works" (2 Timothy 3:16–17), we are well advised to be sure we have used the Q-Tips of prayer and Bible study so that our ears are cleaned out so we are able to hear what the Lord intends for us to hear.

Part II

Selected

Old Testamenmt

One Liners

Notes on Part II

Looking in the Old Testament, we found fewer "One Liners" than we expected, unless you count the dozens of times Scripture repeats, "And the Lord spake unto Moses, saying. . . ." Similar verses are found throughout the Old Testament as God spoke to the various prophets with messages that were to be taken seriously and faithfully by the people they served. When something is repeated so often, there is a reason.

Name dropping is a common thing these days. "Why just yesterday, I had lunch with so-and-so; you remember so-and-so, don't you? Well, she said. . . ." If so-and-so was a movie star, major politician, TV personality, or sports figure, you can be sure the other people involved in the conversation were paying close attention to what came next. When the name of someone well known is dropped, it is guaranteed to get a response.

Moses and the other prophets did not mention God just to elicit a "wow" from the people, but to make it clear that they were not speaking a personal message, but instructions, warnings, or guidance from God Himself. The children of Israel, while traveling through the desert in their forty years of wandering, saw the smoke on the mountain; they heard the thunder; they saw the shining face of Moses; they saw the miracles. They knew that Moses had been with God on Sinai. When he said, "The Lord told me to tell you this," they accepted what he said. They knew he had received the message from God.

Not every prophet was so fortunate. Some were scorned or ignored as though they were speaking for themselves, but just were dropping God's name to get attention. Others were false prophets, who pretended to speak in God's name. Before the written Word was available to all as it is today, it was imperative for the people to be able to discern whether the spokesperson was true or false.

Deuteronomy 18:20–22 gives the litmus test for prophets:

> But the prophet, which shall presume to speak a word in my name, which I have not commanded him to speak, or that shall speak in the name of other gods, even that prophet shall die. And if thou say in thine heart, How shall we know the word which the LORD hath not spoken? When a prophet speaketh in the name of the LORD, if the thing follow not, nor come to pass, that is the thing which the LORD hath not spoken, but the prophet hath spoken it presumptuously: thou shalt not be afraid of him.

One would presume that there were not many times a would-be prophet was stoned! God's simple test was clear: If the prophet said God told him to speak, but what he said did not come to pass, he was not God's man. God protects His Word! In Psalm 138:2, David said: "I will worship toward thy holy temple, and praise thy name for thy lovingkindness and for thy truth: for thou hast magnified thy word above all thy name."

God has placed serious importance to His Name, so much so that one of the Ten Commandments addresses God's Name specifically. Exodus 20:7 commands: "Thou shalt not take the name of the LORD thy God in vain; for the LORD will not hold him guiltless that taketh his name in vain."

There is little wonder that in today's culture we constantly hear people exclaim, "Oh my God," or add the word "damn" to God's Name, or use the matchless name of the Lord Jesus Christ as an expletive. Satan knows how to rub salt into a wound. Since the day he rebelled against the throne of God and His authority, his intention has been to oppose God in every way possible for as long as he has dominion as the prince of the power of this world.

Within the Decalogue, God gave a commandment to protect His name from corruption. He goes further to say that He has magnified His Word above His Name. This is to reinforce the importance that we don't dare say, "Thus saith the Lord . . ." unless the Lord did indeed say it. There are satanically led deceivers in today's world against whom the

Apostle John, in 3 John 7 warned nearly two thousand years ago: "For many deceivers are entered into the world, who confess not that Jesus Christ is come in the flesh. This is a deceiver and an antichrist."

When the Word of the Lord comes, it comes only one way today: from the pages of inspired Scripture. If your pastor or a Bible teacher gets up in the pulpit and says, "God spoke to me this morning, and I am here to tell you what He said," unless he next tells you to turn to a passage of Scripture and reads what God said from it, head for the door.

"And the Lord spake unto Moses, saying. . . ." Direct communication from God's mouth to our ears does not occur today. We have the complete, inspired, sacred Word of God in our King James Bible. If the Lord wants us to know something, we will find it in the pages between Genesis 1 and Revelation 22. The Bible is a sealed book. At the very end of the Revelation comes this warning: "And if any man shall take away from the words of the book of this prophecy, God shall take away his part out of the book of life, and out of the holy city, and from the things which are written in this book" (Revelation 22:19). The Book of Mormon, the Koran, the Sutras, and all of the "sacred" writings of other religions do not have the truth of God within their pages. Only one factual error is enough to disqualify them. One prophecy that did not come true, one incorrect historical location, one contradiction to what the Bible says, just one event predicted that did not happen, and they are out!

Interestingly, almost all of the writings of the religions of today contain little or no legitimate prophecy. A foundational book of a religion today is conspicuously short on prophecy because it is dangerous to predict the future. Sooner or later, the appointed day will come and the truth will be known. For that matter, ask fortune tellers what their percentage of accuracy is. As they pretend to be modern-day prophets, they do not know the future. Only God does. When God's prophet of old thundered forth, "Thus saith the Lord . . ." he knew what he said would come to pass, because as David said, "for thou hast magnified thy word above all thy name."

Genesis 1:1

In the beginning God created the heaven and the earth

Technically, the first verse in the Bible is too long to qualify for our collection of "God's One Liners," but we will make an exception. This verse cannot be ignored because it answers major questions.

It answers when: at the beginning.

It answers Who: God.

It answers what: He made everything.

It has been said that if one can get past the first five words of Genesis, the rest of the Bible will be no problem. For those who choose not to believe it, the major alternative is evolution. All this science fairy tale requires is that you believe there is no firm starting point, that is, no beginning: it just evolved. Bang! Everything came from nothing and no one did it. That makes no sense and takes more faith than the Bible's account of creation!

Foundations. Everything needs them: a building, a family, a nation. One would have a hard time imagining starting to build a home without preparing a firm foundation first. Without a good foundation, only a minimal storm would destroy it. A total loss.

Nearly everyone would agree that a Mercedes Benz is a rather fine automobile. No one would accept the idea that one whipped itself together from spare parts in a junk yard and drove itself away. Much less, no thinking person would suggest that there wasn't even a junk yard, just thin air from which it materialized. Without the foundation of considerable thought and design in the development and engineering, then in the manufacturing and ultimate delivery from the German assembly plant, it would have been impossible to put those vehicles on the show-room floor.

A church is made up of people who have trusted Christ as Savior, and the church needs a foundation, too. As the hymn says, "The Church's one foundation is Jesus Christ, her Lord." The foundational basis for any church is biblical doctrine. Unfortunately, in today's world of compromise and a Rodney King-ish "Can't we all just get along?" mentality, doctrine is being thrown out in favor of whatever remains as the lowest common denominator of beliefs. During much of the past century, mergers between denominations continued at a fast pace. The Purpose Driven movement has added a new dimension to that downward slide. Most churches are "United" something or another. Doctrine is forsaken in favor of unity. Foundations crumble.

The church today is irrelevant in American society. Some believe it will only be a matter of time before it will whimper off into a corner of oblivion. Granted, that will never happen, but no longer does the entertainment industry worry about Christian sensitivities when it scripts its TV programs and movies. They swipe at everything a Bible-believer holds dear. Some TV programs have begun to use the Lord's name in profanity. Very little at first, but soon it will be as common as it is in the workplace.

Satan has carefully chipped away at the foundations so he can undermine the influence of the church and Bible preaching. Modern science, we are told, doesn't need God since He is irrelevant. A large segment of so-called Christianity thinks man is improving conditions on earth so that some day we will hand over the keys to the Lord and tell him, "Okay, you can drive it now. We have it all fixed." On what planet have they been living?

Nevertheless, in the beginning, it was God and only God who spoke, and by the authority of His words the worlds were formed, and, by the way, He did it in six days! It was not six billion years, but six twenty-four–hour periods. Surely a God with that power could create things with apparent age, not requiring gazillions of years to erode river beds or layers of sediment.

Genesis 1:16 uses just a few words to describe a major portion of creation: "And God made two great lights; the greater light to rule the day, and the lesser light to rule the night: he made the stars also." It is almost funny when one reads that verse. God made the sun and the moon: no mean task. Our sun is an average star, not unusual as stars go, but it is only one of billions. It is almost as if the writer had moved on in the narrative and suddenly remembered, "Oh, God made the stars, too." No big deal. It just took a few minutes, He didn't even break a sweat.

If you have ever seen some of the pictures sent back by the Hubble space telescope, you surely have stared in amazement at the colors, the beauty and infinity of the solar systems and star alignments in the universe.

"In the beginning God created the heaven and the earth." That is an amazingly simple statement, but it is so complex that it has confounded the minds of scientists since the first one of them looked up and noticed the movement of the heavenly constellations, the seasons, the variety of life forms, and man himself.

The ultimate foundations were laid by an all wise and loving God. Others followed who through service and devotion were given the task to add to that foundation. Then more and more put their trust in the Lord Jesus Christ to build the church of believers, who will someday be taken to Heaven to be with the Lord for all eternity. The Apostle Paul in 1 Corinthians 3:10 wrote, "According to the grace of God which is given unto me, as a wise masterbuilder, I have laid the foundation, and another buildeth thereon. But let every man take heed how he buildeth thereupon. For other foundation can no man lay than that is laid, which is Jesus Christ."

You and I, friend, are called to work on the building project. We are no longer at the beginning of it, but very close to the end. Our faithfulness to the task will result in others being added to the church that is redeemed by the blood of Christ.

First Peter 2:2-8 describes the church building process this way:

As newborn babes, desire the sincere milk of the word, that ye may grow thereby: If so be ye have tasted that the Lord is gracious. To whom coming, as unto a living stone, disallowed indeed of men, but chosen of God, and precious, Ye also, as lively stones, are built up a spiritual house, an holy priesthood, to offer up spiritual sacrifices, acceptable to God by Jesus Christ. Wherefore also it is contained in the scripture, Behold, I lay in Sion a chief corner stone, elect, precious: and he that believeth on him shall not be confounded. Unto you therefore which believe he is precious: but unto them which be disobedient, the stone which the builders disallowed, the same is made the head of the corner, And a stone of stumbling, and a rock of offence, even to them which stumble at the word, being disobedient: whereunto also they were appointed.

What man makes ultimately deteriorates and crumbles. What God has made will stand forever.

But Noah found grace in the eyes of the Lord

In reality, this verse is one word too long to qualify, but it is too important to ignore, so we will bend the rules. Actually, in the Old Testament section of this book, we will bend the rules several times.

> *Amazing grace, how sweet the sound*
> *That saved a wretch like me . . .*

Amazing is an appropriate word when it comes to grace. John Newton, the writer of the words of that favorite hymn, knew that all too well. As a wicked sinner, he realized his need of God's forgiveness. He came to know that his eternal future would be Hell, as the reality of his sinful condition became palpable enough for him to be able to ignore it no longer.

David, the great king and songwriter of Israel, wrote in Psalm 51:1–4: "Have mercy upon me, O God, according to thy lovingkindness: according unto the multitude of thy tender mercies blot out my transgressions. Wash me thoroughly from mine iniquity, and cleanse me from my sin. For I acknowledge my transgressions: and my sin is ever before me. Against thee, thee only, have I sinned, and done this evil in thy sight: that thou mightest be justified when thou speakest, and be clear when thou judgest."

David knew God's grace in a very real way, as he was forgiven of his great sin with Bathsheba and the murder of her husband. Throughout David's life, he experienced God's grace again and again.

Others who knew God's marvelous grace in the Old Testament would make a formidable list, but for now, as we focus on Noah, we have to realize what it was like in the world of his day. Historically, this was approximately fifteen hundred years after the creation and twenty-five hundred years before Christ came to be our Savior. It was at a time a little more than five hundred years after the death of Adam. There were still people on the earth who knew Adam personally. They spoke with him, knew the story of creation, and their sin and expulsion from the Garden of Eden. They didn't read of it in history books, but they knew what happened from the mouth of those who had the actual experience! We don't know for sure, but Noah may have known Adam and, if so, knew the story firsthand. It must have been Noah who was the source of the information that formed the first five chapters of Genesis leading up to the flood.

One thing we do know is leading up to that, the sin of mankind on the earth had reached such a level within the lifetime of just these two men, Adam and Noah, that God was sorry He had created man. Genesis 6:5–7: "And God saw that the wickedness of man was great in the earth, and that every imagination of the thoughts of his heart was only evil continually. And it repented the LORD that he had made man on the earth, and it grieved him at his heart. And the LORD said, I will destroy man whom I have created from the face of the earth; both man, and beast, and the creeping thing, and the fowls of the air; for it repenteth me that I have made them."

How bad was it? We can't imagine! Or can we? Conditions on earth today are ripe for God's judgment to fall again. Man has no regard for God, whether it is in our court system, which is ruling against the biblical concepts that have guided our nation since its founding; whether a president who is encouraging the homosexual agenda, godless socialism, and Islam's advance; or the man on the street who has no regard for God. America, and for that matter, the rest of the world, is in line for severe judgment.

In Luke 18, Jesus is teaching about an unjust judge. (It seems they have been around for a long time!) Unlike the judges of today who live a protected life away from the common man, the one of whom the Lord spoke became weary of the pleas for justice from one who had been wronged, and he ultimately gave a judgment in her favor. In verses 7 and 8, Jesus added, "And shall not God avenge his own elect, which cry day and night unto him, though he bear long with them? I tell you that he will avenge them speedily. Nevertheless when the Son of man cometh, shall he find faith on the earth?"

The last sentence is an interesting one. The Lord was telling us that things were going to degenerate to the level that before He returns to the earth, it would be difficult to find any believers on the earth. Here is an experiment for you: Next Sunday, while you are driving to church, count how many joggers you see, how many people walking their dogs, how many riding bicycles, playing ball, having brunch at a restaurant, or driving somewhere in clothes that make it obvious that they are not headed to church. Then, compare that to the number of people who are in a Bible-believing, God-honoring church. The proportion will be very lopsided. God is the farthest concept from their minds. He will not be the One they intend to honor and worship on His day.

In a world that was no different than the world of today, we are encouraged to find one family that had not turned away from Jehovah. "But Noah found grace in the eyes of the LORD." When the Lord returns for His redeemed ones, may he find us watching and faithfully serving Him.

Genesis 49:18

I have waited for thy salvation, O Lord

At the beginning of this chapter, ". . . Jacob called unto his sons, and said, Gather yourselves together, that I may tell you that which shall befall you in the last days." He named them one by one and told them what was to be their future, and also the prophetic implication of each of their lives and the lives of their descendants. This "One Liner" is the third verse applied to Dan. These are the three verses: "Dan shall judge his people, as one of the tribes of Israel. Dan shall be a serpent by the way, an adder in the path, that biteth the horse heels, so that his rider shall fall backward. I have waited for thy salvation, O LORD."

Some prophecy scholars believe that from Dan will come the Anti-Christ. We will have to wait until history is written to see if that is true, but the verses here do no harm to that theory. The one who will come to power during the last seven years of human history before Christ's Kingdom is set up could be described as a judge. Surely, the man of sin will be as dangerous as a serpent, and will cause many to fall—not only in battle but spiritually—to the damnation of their souls. Surely, during that Tribulation period, worldwide Jewry and all believers in Christ will be waiting for salvation that can only come when Christ returns to earth at the Mount of Olives to end the wicked and satanically inspired rule of the Antichrist and to set up his righteous thousand-year millennial kingdom.

Exodus 20:13, 14, 15

Thou shalt not kill.
Thou shalt not commit adultery.
Thou shalt not steal.

We can read page after page of Scripture over and over again and never see some things. Maybe you noticed this before: The verses that deal with our relationship with God are long. The verses dealing with our relationships with other people are short.

One possible reason is that we are estranged from God by our sin, and most people, especially in today's world, have no concept of God, His righteousness as compared to our sin, and our ultimate fate as a result of our sin. God, in His infinite patience, takes time to explain why we should honor Him.

That we should not kill, commit adultery, steal, or covet is known deep down in our being. While we may do those things, often not giving a second's thought to the severity of our actions, that still, small voice deep inside is trying to be heard over the din of our lifestyle all the while. Conscience cannot be turned off completely or forever. At some point we have to face the music, the reality that our sins will separate us from God forever. The sad part about the law of God is we are not able to escape the penalties associated with breaking them.

When we are pulled over by a traffic officer for speeding, we hope he might be kind to us and only give us a warning, but by the time we are meeting him face to face, we are already under the heavy hand of the law. Without his mercy, we pay the fine!

When we break God's law, we are condemned to His judgment, and as Ezekiel 18:4b bluntly states: ". . . the soul that sinneth, it shall die." That one "little" sin isn't so bad in our sight, but in the sight of a holy God Who cannot be in the presence of even a "little" sin, that little sin is an insurmountable problem. The Ten Commandments can be likened to a chain. As long as each link in the chain is strong, it will do its job. If one of the links is broken, the whole chain is of no value. We all hope the chain holding the vicious pit bull down the street holds when we walk past his yard. If one of the links has been compromised, the chain could break at his next lunge.

If one of the links in the Ten Commandments, the most basic statement of divine law, is broken by our sin, the whole chain is broken. We don't think of a chain as individual links, but the total length of the chain as a unit designed to hold back that dog. God doesn't see the "little white lie" we tell as anything short of the breaking of the whole law.

If you have come to the point of realizing your sinful state before a holy God, and confessed your sins, and personally accepted the payment made for you by Christ when He died in your place on the cross, you are no longer under the penalty of breaking God's law. Christ died to forgive us of our sins and cleanse us of all unrighteousness.

In 1 John 1:8–10, God lays out the case against us: "If we say that we have no sin, we deceive ourselves, and the truth is not in us. If we confess our sins, he is faithful and just to forgive us our sins, and to cleanse us from all unrighteousness. If we say that we have not sinned, we make him a liar, and his word is not in us."

The good news is in the second half of verse 7: ". . . the blood of Jesus Christ his Son cleanseth us from all sin."

If you have never asked Him to forgive and cleanse you of the sins you have committed against Him, do so now!

Exodus 22:18

Thou shalt not suffer a witch to live

There have been several notable people who have claimed to be witches or warlocks. They seldom claim to worship the devil, but he is still the center of their worship no matter what name they use to identify him.

Exodus continues to lay down the laws that were to define Israel as a unique nation among nations. God's Name was on them as a people. They were His chosen people. He expected more of them than of their national neighbors. Verse 18 is in the middle of a list of rules and regulations that formed the civil law and rules of conduct of a civilized society. Most of them are easy to understand, both in their meaning and the reason they were enacted. This "One Liner" may be a little harder to understand in today's society.

Jeanne Dixon was rather popular in her day. She wrote a newspaper column, was a guest on radio and television, and was quite influential. She didn't ride a broom. She didn't wear a black robe and a long pointed hat. And, she didn't have a wart on her nose. Satan has cleverly turned a witch into a cartoonish character to help us keep our guard down.

The witch, the Satan worshippers, or whatever you wish to call them, were condemned by God. They are subtle. They pretend to know the future. Go to a county fair or carnival and Madame Hermione will gladly tell your fortune for a small fee. Funny thing, while many people will plunk down the five dollars requested and think of it as entertaining and fun, when the prediction comes true, they may be hooked. "You will meet a tall, dark stranger in the next week." Wow! Who could have ever guessed! The next day, new to your route, a handsome UPS driver delivers a package. Maybe the Madame said, "You will receive money you didn't expect." That could be as simple as getting a refund in the mail for overpaying a bill. Never mind that the "fortune" was a glowing generality that could be true of anyone who lives and breathes on the earth; it came true. The next step will be easier. Before anyone is the wiser, the horoscopes, the Ouija board, the tarot cards, and the palm readings are the normal means of making decisions, leaving God and His Word out of the picture altogether.

If we are not following God and His Word, we are following something or someone else. Ultimately, Satan is that one.

Satan is not capable of knowing the future, but he can manipulate events. Since he is the enemy of our souls, he makes it his regular business to mislead, fool, and cause us mortal humans to fall into one trap after another. If he can speed up the process of our being led astray, he will. In many societies, especially where the people are superstitious, he has used the witch to great advantage.

Within God's order of society for His chosen people, He was setting up a safeguard—a fence, if you will—to keep His people safe from harm. If someone within the Jewish community was found out to be a witch, that one was to be put to death. Capital punishment is a good thing. 1) It solves the immediate problem of the individual law breaker. 2) It removes the influence of the miscreant from the young or gullible. 3) It serves to help others to stay away from the sin that could take them to the same destiny.

Just as you and your neighbors would not want a child molester to live in a neighborhood full of young children, for the same reason, God stipulated that those who would lead people astray from His Word should be kept at a minimum. Common sense requires that poison be kept from those who may be harmed. God is the author of common sense. You can read pages of it in the Bible.

Thou shalt not eat any abominable thing

There has been more than one smarty-pants child that has pointed to this verse when told to eat his broccoli, brussels sprouts or spinach. Sorry, sonny, that is not what is in view here!

One of the most memorable characters in the New Testament is the Apostle Peter. Whatever words you want to use to describe him, shy or backward would not be among them. He was the undeclared leader. He spoke out and stepped out time after time. When he was presented with a feast of lobster, shrimp, bacon, clams, and who knows what else, Peter said, "No-siree! Not me. Uh-uh! Not that stuff. I don't eat unclean cuisine." Well, he didn't say it quite like that, but that is what Peter's words in Acts 10 would translate to in everyday language when he was called to carry the gospel message to the gentiles.

This writer, for one, can think of few things more delicious than Dungeness crab, king crab legs, shrimp scampi, and best of all, lobstars! Yes, the proper spelling is lobster, but on my table, they would be the stars of any dinner. Some folks who do not follow a kosher diet will still avoid pork products and shellfish. That is okay. They have to follow their conscience before the Lord. Many believe that we are free to eat whatever we wish in the age of grace in which we live. Proper preparation and sanitation, safe fertilizers, and careful inspection have made many foods safe to eat compared to a time in the past.

First Corinthians 10 deals with foods that may bring offence to others, and is recommended reading. Dear Reader, please be careful not to use your liberty as a cause for another to stumble, nor as a club over the head of someone who may not agree with you.

Animals from shrimp to swine, eels to eagles, and even eggs are capable of causing major disease outbreaks wherever they are not properly handled and prepared. God knew this. He set up a list of types of animals that were not to be eaten for the protection of His people. In the Old Testament, diet was very important in a nomadic society as at the time of the Exodus. The temptation might have been to eat anything they could catch in the wild. An epidemic could have ensued.

Today, we raise pigs, catfish, shrimp, and many other "bottom feeders" in farms with carefully controlled water, sanitation, and nutrients to insure the food is safe to eat. Such was not the case several thousand years ago. In some parts of the world, many things are not safe to eat even today, including some plant crops that have been in the news in recent months because of salmonella or other harmful bacteria.

The dietary laws followed by observant Jews, the laws of kosher, are not foolproof for preventing problems, but they provided a protective fence around the people. Those laws surely are the answer in many cases where people have problems with certain foods. If this is something about which you have a concern, pray for the Lord to guide you to know His will. There is not a contradiction between 1 Corinthians 10 and Deuteronomy 14. They are written for different times in God's dispensational dealing with man.

Of all clean birds ye shall eat

Similar to the verse above, this verse is part of a passage intended to give guidance to God's people as they formed the nation of Israel, having come out of Egypt where many things were tolerated that God despised. God didn't remove everything from His people, just those things He knew would cause problems.

His mercy toward us today is the same. He allows us many things richly to enjoy, as 1 Timothy 6:17 mentions, while at the same time, prohibiting what He knows will do harm.

Blessed shall be thy basket and thy store

In Deuteronomy 28:1–2, Moses is telling the children of Israel about the plans God has for them: "And it shall come to pass, if thou shalt hearken diligently unto the voice of the LORD thy God, to observe and to do all his commandments which I command thee this day, that the LORD thy God will set thee on high above all nations of the earth: And all these blessings shall come on thee, and overtake thee, if thou shalt hearken unto the voice of the LORD thy God."

In return for their faithfulness, His blessings on them would include every aspect of life: family, cities, fields, crops, travel. They would enjoy God's protection from enemies, and blessings untold.

Just a few verses later is a mirror image of the beginning of the chapter. Here God warns that they would face hardships if they forsook Him. Verses 14 and following spell out potential curses on them for un-faithfulness: "And thou shalt not go aside from any of the words which I command thee this day, to the right hand, or to the left, to go after other gods to serve them. But it shall come to pass, if thou wilt not hearken unto the voice of the LORD thy God, to observe to do all his commandments and his statutes which I command thee this day; that all these curses shall come upon thee, and overtake thee: Cursed shalt thou be in the city, and cursed shalt thou be in the field. Cursed shall be thy basket and thy store."

During the course of the Old Testament's history, we saw both the blessings and the curses come to Israel as they allowed the pendulum to swing from faithfulness to faithlessness. What might have happened if Israel had held faithful throughout their history? What if they had accepted the Lord Jesus as their Messiah-Christ? Alas, it didn't happen.

What about our lives? These promises were made to Israel but can be claimed by a believer today. God delights in blessing His children, but He will take us to the woodshed for discipline when it is required.

Psalm 16:1

Preserve me, O God:
for in thee do I put my trust

The Psalms are full of favorite verses. No wonder, as so many of them are uplifting and hopeful. Certainly that is not true of all of them, but many.

After Samuel anointed him king, David spent a considerable amount of time keeping distance from King Saul. His life depended on it! No wonder we read "Preserve me, O God" as the first portion of this psalm. Instead of wallowing in his concerns for his life, he quickly turns to praise, as seen in the last four verses: "I have set the LORD always before me: because he is at my right hand, I shall not be moved. Therefore my heart is glad, and my glory rejoiceth: my flesh also shall rest in hope. For thou wilt not leave my soul in hell; neither wilt thou suffer thine Holy One to see corruption. Thou wilt shew me the path of life: in thy presence is fulness of joy; at thy right hand there are pleasures for evermore."

I will love thee, O Lord, my strength

David is still concerned for his life in this psalm, but again his attention is on the goodness of his God. His love for the Lord is clearly evident as David remembers different things about the Lord for which he is thankful.

"The LORD is my rock, and my fortress, and my deliverer; my God, my strength, in whom I will trust; my buckler, and the horn of my salvation, and my high tower. I will call upon the LORD, who is worthy to be praised: so shall I be saved from mine enemies" (vss. 2–3).

David focused on the strength of the Lord, then in verse 6, he is thankful for a God who is a prayer-hearing/answering God: "In my distress I called upon the LORD, and cried unto my God: he heard my voice out of his temple, and my cry came before him, even into his ears."

Another familiar verse often put to music is verse 46: "The LORD liveth; and blessed be my rock; and let the God of my salvation be exalted." David's reliance was not on his own efforts, but solely upon God for his salvation.

We can take a great example from David. When things get tough, focus on the Lord and His goodness. Suddenly, as the old hymn lyric says, "And the things of earth will grow strangely dim in the light of His glory and grace."

Psalm 23:1

The Lord is my shepherd;
I shall not want

There are few more memorized portions of scripture than Psalm 23. As a shepherd himself, David is clearly aware that it is the shepherd's responsibility to meet the needs of his sheep. A sheep lacks intelligence. It would starve if it had to find its own food. It could never find its way home if lost. It surely cannot defend itself against enemies.

Other than being very cute when small, one of the few things to endear a sheep to its shepherd is the fact that it recognizes his voice and will respond to his call.

Jesus said in John 10:27–28: "My sheep hear my voice, and I know them, and they follow me: And I give unto them eternal life; and they shall never perish, neither shall any man pluck them out of my hand."

David had a relationship with his Shepherd that assured him that his every need would be met, and because he followed his great Shepherd, he could look forward to dwelling in God's Heaven for ever.

That promise is ours today, as well!

Unto thee, O Lord, do I lift up my soul

Several times in this psalm, David asks God to not remember his transgressions (vs. 7), his iniquities (vs. 11), and his sins (vs. 18), all synonyms for sin. He had learned a lesson the hard way: sin—public or private—will eventually become revealed and will cause shame for the sinner and often serious consequences for the sinner as well as others.

David's concern here is that his shame would not lead to his enemies having opportunity to gain victory over him or be able to malign the name of the Lord. Verses 2 and 20 are very similar: David's trust is solely in the Lord.

God is known in her palaces
for a refuge

Psalm 48 was a song of praise to God extolling the beauty of Jerusalem, the capital of Israel, and prophetically, the city where the "great King" would reign (v.2).

The late prophecy teacher, J. R. Church, produced an interesting book some years back showing that the Psalms (the nineteenth book in the progression of the books of the Bible) represented the years of the same number throughout the century known as the 1900s. Accordingly, Psalm 48 represented the year 1948—the year Israel was declared a nation by the United Nations.

Verses 11–14 seem to be prophetic: "Let mount Zion rejoice, let the daughters of Judah be glad, because of thy judgments. Walk about Zion, and go round about her: tell the towers thereof. Mark ye well her bulwarks, consider her palaces; that ye may tell it to the generation following. For this God is our God for ever and ever: he will be our guide even unto death."

The allusion to "the generation following" is thought by some to mean that the generation that experienced the reestablishment of Israel as a nation would grow up to be the last generation before Christ's return as the Jewish Messiah. We will have to wait and see. There is reason to have hope that this will be reality. The signs of Christ's imminent return are many!

Psalm 92:8

But thou, Lord, art most high for evermore

David was truly in love with his Lord. There was no holding back of his devotion and admiration for Him. Just as one's spouse, child, or parent loves to be told he is loved, so too, does the Lord. We love to hear someone say good things about us. So does the Lord. When we give testimony of the Lord's goodness at church, work, or in our families, we can know the Lord is smiling, just as we would enjoy hearing our praises being sung.

While someone who is ignorant, wicked, an evildoer, or a fool cannot appreciate fine things, and may even be destructive of them, David acknowledges that God is high and holy over and over again, giving us some of the rationale he has for his praise.

In today's society, if we have even basic common sense, we would not antagonize an officer of the law; we would not pick a fight with someone twice our size; and certainly we would not post on a Facebook page that we were going to do some act of violence. We surely would face the music if we did. David recognizes that "all the workers of iniquity shall be scattered" (vs. 9).

Why does David praise the most high God? He has found from a personal walk with Him that He is trustworthy, praiseworthy, and worthy of worship because "there is no unrighteousness in him" (vs. 15).

Psalm 109:1

Hold not thy peace,
O God of my praise

Again, we have a psalm written at a time when David was being opposed by those who were not led of God. Wicked, lying adversaries were turning his good works into evil.

What could David do? As king, he had an army of faithful warriors. He could send them into battle to defeat his enemies. It would not be the first time he did so. He could mount a campaign of lies and innuendo against them, matching point for point with his rebuttal, much like we see among our politicians. He could send in double agents to undermine the efforts of the opposition. He could . . .

He did not do any of those things. In verse 1, we see David is praying. Looking at the middle verses of this psalm, we see some of the strongest language ever placed in Scripture. An imprecation is a prayer for God to judge one who is unrighteous. This is not a prayer to be offered lightly, since God could not be expected to honor such a prayer if inappropriate. God might even be of a mind to turn the tables and bring down His wrath on the one who was asking Him to judge another if it was not a legitimate prayer.

Obviously, from his prayer, we know there was major opposition to David's kingdom. Keeping in mind that ALL scripture is inspired, God wants us to know what David prayed and to know it is all right for us to pray such a prayer when it is appropriate.

When is it appropriate? When there is wickedness at every hand;

when evil seems to be winning and God's Word and will are being ignored, maligned, and trampled; when there is outright and gross sin in plain view, God expects us to cry out to Him for an end to that sin. He has promised that He will judge the abominations of man with finality.

When we see openly flaunted homosexuality in the streets during Mardi Gras or gay pride festivals, when it is elevated to preferred status within our government, we know God stands against it (Romans 1:18–32). We are justified in praying for God to judge and remove the wicked influence before it extends further, thereby causing harm to more and more lives.

God wants us to agree with Him in prayer about what is sin and what is godly, and He wants us to seek His face for His will to be done. In Matthew 18:19, Christ is telling His disciples, "Again I say unto you, That if two of you shall agree on earth as touching any thing that they shall ask, it shall be done for them of my Father which is in heaven." In the Lord's Prayer, the line "Thy will be done in earth, as it is in heaven" comes to mind. Surely the sins of our day are not in Heaven. Praying for HIS will is our responsibility. His responsibility is to answer as He sees fit, when He sees fit.

When children from kindergarten age are being influenced to accept the unacceptable, it is time to pray for the removal of those who are promoting sin.

When drugs invade a neighborhood to the point safety is only a word, it is time to pray.

When crime—murder, rape, robbery, assault, and plunder—is the rule of the day and always the lead story on the evening news, it is time to pray.

When abortion takes the lives of millions of innocent lives while many think nothing of even the most abhorrent methods involved, it is time to pray.

When protests, elections, and public awareness have not been strong enough to turn the tide, it is time to pray. It is time to pray that God will intervene as He sees fit.

Psalm 116:11

I said in my haste,
All men are liars

Either Hezekiah or David is believed to have been the writer of this psalm. As one reads it, there are a number of verses that may be familiar, even memorized. The first eight verses are filled with praise to the Lord; the last half of the psalm is praise and assurance of the Lord's presence and salvation.

Then, there is verse 11. It seems to be a disconnect from the rest of the psalm.

Verses 9–11 say, "I will walk before the Lord in the land of the living. I believed, therefore have I spoken: I was greatly afflicted: I said in my haste, All men are liars."

In effect, the writer is saying, *On one hand we have God and His faithfulness and mercy. On the other hand is man, who is untrustworthy.* All of us have seen this comparison in life. People we trust are bound to disappoint us. Just wait until someone dies and see what happens when the will is probated and someone thinks he has not gotten his fair share.

Apparently the writer had spoken a message from the Lord but it was not well received. Understatement! He was lied about and persecuted for it.

Paul wrote in Romans 14:16, "Let not then your good be evil spoken of . . ." and it seems our psalmist understood that concept. Instead of dwelling on the negatives, in verse 12 he returns to his praise of the Lord asking rhetorically, "What shall I render unto the LORD for all his benefits toward me?"

News flash: Man can't be trusted, but God can! Now, how can I thank Him properly? The rest of the psalm answers the question, going so far as to consider his giving of thanks as a sacrificial offering. "I will offer to thee the sacrifice of thanksgiving, and will call upon the name of the LORD" (vs. 17). At first glance, that seems odd, but when we think about it, a sacrificial offering is something of value that we bring to God.

How much we love the Lord will show itself in what we give to Him. Time, devotion, service, praise, and thanksgiving would be of higher value to Him than our money. When we give from the depths of our spirit those intangible offerings that show our love for Him, His Name is honored more than if we put a fat check in the offering plate.

In verses 18–19, he says, "I will pay my vows unto the LORD now in the presence of all his people, In the courts of the LORD's house, in the midst of thee, O Jerusalem." Can you visualize someone sitting in the middle of the church with a look of dread on his face as the offering plate approaches his position, finally reaching into his wallet, taking out a crumpled dollar bill, and with a scowl on his brow throwing it into the offering plate? It would send a message that would be loud and clear. There was no joy in that offering.

The psalmist is clearly glad to sacrifice his praise as well as possessions to the Lord, not to be a show-off, but so that all who may see it will know it is done with joy. He was a living declaration of the last four words of the psalm: "Praise ye the Lord!"

Psalm 119:113

I hate vain thoughts:
but thy law do I love

Psalm 119 is the longest psalm in the Bible. One hundred and seventy-six verses long, it is divided into twenty-two stanzas of eight verses each. Each stanza is coupled with a letter of the Hebrew aleph beth. (We call it the alphabet.) Each verse has a reference to the law, word, commandments, testimonies, statutes, precepts, or another word that is synonymous with the Old Testament law, the Torah.

Virtually all of the verses are short, but only one is short enough to be considered a "One Liner." This is a contrast verse. In the first phrase the writer declares that he hates vain thoughts. He has no use for worthless chatter. Facebook, the Internet, and text messaging had not yet been invented. They have their value, but surely he could have included them, as so much on them is of little worth.

The second phrase contrasts directly and balances the first. He declares that he loves God's law. If we took an inventory of all the things we think about in a day, how many of them would be vain? By contrast, how much time do we spend meditating on the Word of God? A little time spent considering our thoughts could prove valuable for all of eternity!

Psalm 126:5

They that sow in tears shall reap in joy

If we consider verse 6 with verse 5, we get a bit more continuity of thought: "They that sow in tears shall reap in joy. He that goeth forth and weepeth, bearing precious seed, shall doubtless come again with rejoicing, bringing his sheaves with him."

A farmer plants his seed and waits for the rain. If the rain doesn't come, or if not enough comes, he has a crop failure. Seeds do not germinate and grow to produce crops if they are not watered or if drought comes after they have started to grow. In many areas of the country, one will see extensive watering systems that spray water on the growing fields when there is not enough rain. As long as a drought is not severe, the water will be enough to bridge the gap between rainstorms. The tremendous drought in the southwestern portion of the United States during the summer of 2011 was severe enough that the wells tapped for the watering went dry. The farmlands became a dust bowl, as in the past when all was lost.

Three of the Gospel writers tell the parable of the sower given as an object lesson by the Lord. In Luke 8:11, Jesus answers the disciples request for an explanation of the parable related in the previous verses by telling them that the seed sowed by the farmer represents the Word of God. The method employed for sowing in those days, and still used in many undeveloped areas today, was broadcasting. That is to say, the farmer would take a handful of seed and toss it across the field. Modern farm equipment was still centuries away from being invented.

When the farmer tossed the seed, some of it would fall on the way-side, some on the top of a rock, some into a tangle of thorns, but, one would hope, most of it would fall on good, well-prepared ground. Jesus compared the types of ground to the people who would hear the Word when it was preached. Some would reject it outright. Others would listen and give assent to it, but there would be no spiritual growth.

Others would hear it, start to grow, and be nourished by the Word, but later be drawn away by false doctrine, discouragement, or the cares of life. They started well, but never reached the finish line in service to the Lord.

While in today's world it seems as though the majority of those who hear the Word do not respond or do not show more than a momentary interest, there are those who accept the truth with gladness and "grow in grace, and in the knowledge of our Lord and Saviour Jesus Christ" (2 Peter 3:18).

The water needed for seed to germinate has been compared to the tears that one might shed in love and concern for the lost. If we have a true grasp of the horror of an eternal existence in the lake of fire, separated from loved ones, but much worse, separated from God for all eternity, it should move us to compassion. Surely there have been countless parents or spouses who have shed rivers of tears while imploring the Lord to save their loved one. Truly, when that loved one finally comes to faith in Jesus Christ, the tears that were sown will bring forth a harvest of joy!

It has been said that the only thing we can take to Heaven is another person. We can't take our riches. They will stay behind when we die. Our worldly accomplishments, even a Nobel Prize or some other great honor, will not even be remembered in Heaven. Even if we had the proper mailing address, we would not be able to send anything in advance other than those who have been won to the Savior by our witness. What a wonderful thing it will be when we get to Heaven's shore to see those who trusted in Christ because we were faithful in our witness for Him.

And the idols he shall utterly abolish

While an idol can be a statue that people bow down before to worship, it can also be anything that replaces God in a person's life. It can be another person, a possession, a position. It can be money or a personal goal. It can be self.

David said in Psalm 42:1, "As the hart panteth after the water brooks, so panteth my soul after thee, O God." That is a strong statement. Would many of us say the same today? David had ups and downs in his life, but he always turned back to God in true repentance when he was aware of his sin. Whatever got in the way of David's relationship with God was removed as quickly as possible.

Fast-forward some years to the time of Isaiah and he is telling of the future when "the LORD's house shall be established in the top of the mountains, and shall be exalted above the hills; and all nations shall flow unto it" (Isaiah 2:2). It will be a day of purification as the things that "so easily beset us" will be gone. It will be a day of great blessing for, as verse 17 tells, "the LORD alone shall be exalted in that day."

All of the things that are evil, sinful, and maybe even the things that are fattening will be done away with. All of the things that man has elevated to a level of importance that conflict with God's plan will be gone.

It will be a day of great wonder and blessing when we see Christ face to face and everything that ever got in the way of our fellowship with Him will be forever removed.

Comfort ye, comfort ye my people, saith your God

Isaiah 40:1–9 contains verses, and portions of verses, very familiar to anyone who has sung or heard Handel's great oratorio, "Messiah." If you know it, you will surely hear the melodies in your mind as you read these verses:

Comfort ye, comfort ye my people, saith your God. Speak ye comfortably to Jerusalem, and cry unto her, that her warfare is accomplished, that her iniquity is pardoned: for she hath received of the LORD's hand double for all her sins. The voice of him that crieth in the wilderness, Prepare ye the way of the LORD, make straight in the desert a highway for our God. Every valley shall be exalted, and every mountain and hill shall be made low: and the crooked shall be made straight, and the rough places plain: And the glory of the LORD shall be revealed, and all flesh shall see it together: for the mouth of the LORD hath spoken it. The voice said, Cry. And he said, What shall I cry? All flesh is grass, and all the goodliness thereof is as the flower of the field: The grass withereth, the flower fadeth: because the spirit of the LORD bloweth upon it: surely the people is grass. The grass withereth, the flower fadeth: but the word of our God shall stand for ever. O Zion, that bringest good tidings, get thee up into the high mountain; O Jerusalem, that bringest good tidings, lift up thy voice with strength; lift it up, be not afraid; say unto the cities of Judah, Behold your God!

When a loved one passes from this life, comfort may be hard to find or to accept when offered by others, even if the deceased loved one knew and walked with the Savior. Human nature cannot be tossed aside: Death brings about loss and loneliness for the ones left behind. The loss of a loved one is a very personal thing.

For the Jew of the past, Jerusalem was the holy city. It was the ultimate destination. More than once, disobedient Israel was forced from the land and there was great mourning, but on a day future, when Messiah comes, there will be comfort.

In John 19:13–16 we have the account of the day of Christ's crucifixion:

> When Pilate therefore heard that saying, he brought Jesus forth, and sat down in the judgment seat in a place that is called the Pavement, but in the Hebrew, Gabbatha. And it was the preparation of the passover, and about the sixth hour: and he saith unto the Jews, Behold your King! But they cried out, Away with him, away with him, crucify him. Pilate saith unto them, Shall I crucify your King? The chief priests answered, We have no king but Caesar. Then delivered he him therefore unto them to be crucified. And they took Jesus, and led him away.

Pilate said, "Behold your king." The people said, "We don't want Him."

Forty years later, the temple was destroyed and the Jews were again dispersed to other lands until the movement back to the land began a little over one hundred years ago.

Some day future, the cry will be, "Behold your God!" and He will be accepted. That day may not be too far in the future, and it will be a wonderful day!

Isaiah 42:18

Hear, ye deaf; and look, ye blind, that ye may see

Hear Him, ye deaf, His praise ye dumb;
Your loosened tongues employ!
Ye blind, behold your Savior comes,
And leap ye lame for joy!

These great words from the hymn "O For a Thousand Tongues to Sing" may have had their inspiration in this verse in Isaiah 42.

In the context, from verse 16 to verse 20, we read:

And I will bring the blind by a way that they knew not; I will lead them in paths that they have not known: I will make darkness light before them, and crooked things straight. These things will I do unto them, and not forsake them. They shall be turned back, they shall be greatly ashamed, that trust in graven images, that say to the molten images, Ye are our gods. Hear, ye deaf; and look, ye blind, that ye may see. Who is blind, but my servant? or deaf, as my messenger that I sent? who is blind as he that is perfect, and blind as the LORD'S servant? Seeing many things, but thou observest not; opening the ears, but he heareth not.

It is easy not to see the forest for the trees, as the old idiom goes, and that seems to be the issue before us in these verses. God wants His people to follow him into blessing, but blindness is the handicap here.

It was Paul who wrote in Romans 11:25, "For I would not, brethren, that ye should be ignorant of this mystery, lest ye should be wise in your own conceits; that blindness in part is happened to Israel, until the fulness of the Gentiles be come in."

In Romans 10:1, one can hear Paul's burden: "Brethren, my heart's desire and prayer to God for Israel is, that they might be saved." It is not unheard of, but it is unusual for a Jewish person to accept the Lord Jesus as Messiah.

That will change on a future day foretold in Zechariah 12:10 when God says: "And I will pour upon the house of David, and upon the inhabitants of Jerusalem, the spirit of grace and of supplications: and they shall look upon me whom they have pierced, and they shall mourn for him, as one mourneth for his only son, and shall be in bitterness for him, as one that is in bitterness for his firstborn."

Isaiah 57:21

*There is no peace, saith
my God, to the wicked*

For the sake of context, we will go back to verse 15 where God declares His holiness, and thus, His qualifications to be God.

> For thus saith the high and lofty One that inhabiteth eternity, whose name is Holy; I dwell in the high and holy place, with him also that is of a contrite and humble spirit, to revive the spirit of the humble, and to revive the heart of the contrite ones. For I will not contend for ever, neither will I be always wroth: for the spirit should fail before me, and the souls which I have made. For the iniquity of his covetousness was I wroth, and smote him: I hid me, and was wroth, and he went on frowardly in the way of his heart. I have seen his ways, and will heal him: I will lead him also, and restore comforts unto him and to his mourners. I create the fruit of the lips; Peace, peace to him that is far off, and to him that is near, saith the LORD; and I will heal him. But the wicked are like the troubled sea, when it cannot rest, whose waters cast up mire and dirt. There is no peace, saith my God, to the wicked.

The promise of an eternity with the holy Creator God of the universe is an incredible thing to consider. If an envelope arrived with the unmistakable return address of The White House, 1600 Pennsylvania Avenue, Washington, D.C., it is safe to imagine it would create quite a stir at your house, whether the current occupant of it was a favorite or not.

When opened, if it contained a personally signed invitation to meet and spend the evening with the President of the United States, it is safe to say a chain of events would follow that would include clearing anything on the schedule that might conflict, new clothes, hair appointments, brush-ups on protocol, and more than a few times of re-reading the letter just to be sure it really said what you thought it did. There would be anxious anticipation and expectation as the date approached.

Now, compare that with this: The Lord of glory invites us to spend not just an evening, but all of eternity with Him in His incredible Heaven! "I dwell in the high and holy place, with him also that is of a contrite and humble spirit. . . ." The one who has realized his sinfulness and confessed it before God, accepting the salvation He offers, qualifies for that incredible future.

The "high and holy place" has never seen sin within its boundaries since Satan and one-third of the angels rebelled. The ones who will dwell there with God will have been cleansed and purified. First Corinthians 15:49–54 is a fantastic passage and is almost beyond comprehension:

> And as we have borne the image of the earthy, we shall also bear the image of the heavenly. Now this I say, brethren, that flesh and blood cannot inherit the kingdom of God; neither doth corruption inherit incorruption. Behold, I shew you a mystery; We shall not all sleep, but we shall all be changed, In a moment, in the twinkling of an eye, at the last trump: for the trumpet shall sound, and the dead shall be raised incorruptible, and we shall be changed. For this corruptible must put on incorruption, and this mortal must put on immortality. So when this corruptible shall have put on incorruption, and this mortal shall have put on immortality, then shall be brought to pass the saying that is written, Death is swallowed up in victory.

When Christ takes His bride (those who have put their trust in Him for their forgiveness of sin, for their personal salvation) to Heaven, there will be a total makeover. New body, new desires, new appearance, new vitality, no more scars, gray hair, or false teeth. We will be changed! We will no longer be mortal human flesh. Even better, the human nature that makes us want to sin will be gone!

"Death is swallowed up in victory." What a wonderful concept. It doesn't just tell us to stop worrying about death, but it assures us that death is a totally conquered foe. There will be peace and victory over every enemy. But wait! We are getting ahead of ourselves. The focus of these thoughts is not the victory of that future day when Jesus comes to Rapture us from this life.

Those who have not placed their faith and complete trust in the Lord Jesus Christ will not even get a glimpse of that peace or victory. Isaiah 59:1–3 paints a completely different picture: "Behold, the LORD's hand is not shortened, that it cannot save; neither his ear heavy, that it cannot hear: But your iniquities have separated between you and your God, and your sins have hid his face from you, that he will not hear. For your hands are defiled with blood, and your fingers with iniquity; your lips have spoken lies, your tongue hath muttered perverseness."

But . . . You could have . . . But . . . But the wicked . . . But your iniquities . . . Someone long ago penned the words, "The saddest words of tongue or pen . . . It might have been." Sin separates. It separates friends, husbands and wives, children, parents, neighbors. That separation may be willful lack of contact or it may be divorce, imprisonment, or even death. Our sin is the barrier between us and God that even God Himself cannot take down. He did all He could to make it possible to remove it from us, as far as the east is from the west, when Christ took our sins on Himself and died in our place, but not even God can take that sin away from us without our asking Him to do so. He gives us the choice to have our sins forgiven, but no matter how much He loves us and wants us to turn to Him, He will not force His will on us.

There are untold millions on planet Earth who have heard that God loves them and wants them to be His child through faith in Christ, but . . . hearing is not enough. They must make the first move. They must ask for the forgiveness.

"But the wicked are like the troubled sea, when it cannot rest, whose waters cast up mire and dirt. There is no peace, saith my God, to the wicked."

Most people recoil at the thought of being called wicked, but what else can we be when compared to a pure and holy God? We must see ourselves as God sees us before we can become what God wants to see when He sees us.

Until we recognize our condition, we have no hope. If you have ever been at one of our seacoasts after a major storm churned up the shoreline, you know how much debris can be scattered on the sand. Hurricane Irene did that in August 2011, and this writer saw firsthand the mess, not only on the shore, but still in the water, sloshing back and forth with the waves that had gone far beyond their normal boundaries, just waiting for the next tide to carry it to shore. It is not a pretty sight. The storm destroying all within its path is not a picture of peace.

Those who are in the path of a hurricane or tornado do not typically lie back in their easy chair to take a nap. Tension is high; fear and uncertainty are the order of the moment. There is no peace.

The unsaved person, even though seemingly enjoying life, may never admit it, but he knows the future is something to fear. God has placed within each of us a conscience that accuses us of our sin like a prosecuting attorney. We may ultimately develop a deaf ear and turn off that still small voice, or we can heed it. It is a personal choice. God will not force His will upon us.

It is bad enough to live with fear and the lack of peace, but God's Word has yet one more thing to say to make leaving this life without God's salvation that much more frightening. Revelation 20:10–15 paints a terrible picture:

> And the devil that deceived them was cast into the lake of fire and brimstone, where the beast and the false prophet are, and shall be tormented day and night for ever and ever. And I saw a great white throne, and him that sat on it, from whose face the earth and the heaven fled away; and there was found no place for them. And I saw the dead, small and great, stand before God; and the books were opened: and another book was opened, which is the book of life: and the dead were judged out of those things which were written in the books, according to their works. And the sea gave up the dead which were in it; and death and hell delivered up the dead which were in them: and they were judged every man according to their works. And death and hell were cast into the lake of fire. This is the second death.

And whosoever was not found written in the book of life was cast into the lake of fire.

Why is there no peace for the wicked? There is the answer. The biblical description of Hell is bad enough. Add to the ultimate reality of Hell, Satan and all his fallen angels as its primary residents, and all whose names were not in the book of life being cast into the lake of fire. To suffer a burn is painful. To spend all of eternity in liquid fire with no hope of an end of it is impossible to comprehend. But it is possible to avoid.

First John, the little letter written by the Apostle John, found near the end of the Bible says this:

This then is the message which we have heard of him, and declare unto you, that God is light, and in him is no darkness at all. If we say that we have fellowship with him, and walk in darkness, we lie, and do not the truth: But if we walk in the light, as he is in the light, we have fellowship one with another, and the blood of Jesus Christ his Son cleanseth us from all sin. If we say that we have no sin, we deceive ourselves, and the truth is not in us. If we confess our sins, he is faithful and just to forgive us our sins, and to cleanse us from all unrighteousness. If we say that we have not sinned, we make him a liar, and his word is not in us.

—1 John 1:5–10

Later, in chapter 3, verse 8, we read: "He that committeth sin is of the devil; for the devil sinneth from the beginning. For this purpose the Son of God was manifested, that he might destroy the works of the devil."

Chapter 4, verses 8–10 further explains: "He that loveth not knoweth not God; for God is love. In this was manifested the love of God toward us, because that God sent his only begotten Son into the world, that we might live through him. Herein is love, not that we loved God, but that he loved us, and sent his Son to be the propitiation for our sins." And in chapter 5, verses 11–13: "And this is the record, that God hath given to us eternal life, and this life is in his Son. He that hath the Son hath life; and he that hath not the Son of God hath not life. These things have I written unto you that believe on the name of the Son of God; that ye may know that ye have eternal life, and that ye may believe on the name of the Son of God."

There is hope. His name is Jesus. "Believe on the Lord Jesus Christ, and thou shalt be saved" (Acts 16:31).

Ephraim is joined to idols: let him alone

I wash my hands of Ephraim! Why?

At the beginning of chapter 4, we read:

> Hear the word of the LORD, ye children of Israel: for the LORD hath
> a controversy with the inhabitants of the land, because there is no
> truth, nor mercy, nor knowledge of God in the land. By swearing, and
> lying, and killing, and stealing, and committing adultery, they break
> out, and blood toucheth blood. Therefore shall the land mourn, and
> every one that dwelleth therein shall languish, with the beasts of the
> field, and with the fowls of heaven; yea, the fishes of the sea also shall
> be taken away.

This is a description of Israel at a very low ebb in her history. No one
would be able to tell that this was the nation God had chosen from all
of the others to bless and to lead. It would be nearly impossible not
to draw a parallel between Israel at the time of Hosea and the United
States today. While not indicating the warning is specifically for the
U.S.A., there are principles here that cannot be ignored by any nation
or government. More than any other nation on the face of the earth, at
any time in history, the U.S.A. has been blessed with the abundance of
everything we could desire. Even those classified as poor among us are
rich by the standards of the rest of the world.

Why? At the risk of having an answer that is too simplistic, it is because from the foundation of the earliest colonies, there was a desire to have the God of the Bible at the head of our nation. Nearly all of the people who came to these shores were looking for freedom from tyranny, freedom to have a voice in their destiny without despotic rule, and freedom to worship God as their consciences dictated.

Charters, state constitutions, and countless other public documents have consistently acknowledged faith in, and dependence on, Divine Providence as the hope of those who were establishing government. This is true to the extent that the United States was known as a Christian nation for more than two centuries until Mr. Obama declared that we are a multireligious nation, which includes Islam within its foundational heritage. Clear examination would declare that nothing could be further from the truth!

Hosea 4:6–10 continues the charges against Israel of old and can also be applied very easily to the United States at this time in history:

> My people are destroyed for lack of knowledge: because thou hast rejected knowledge, I will also reject thee, that thou shalt be no priest to me: seeing thou hast forgotten the law of thy God, I will also forget thy children. As they were increased, so they sinned against me: therefore will I change their glory into shame. They eat up the sin of my people, and they set their heart on their iniquity. And there shall be, like people, like priest: and I will punish them for their ways, and reward them their doings. For they shall eat, and not have enough: they shall commit whoredom, and shall not increase: because they have left off to take heed to the LORD.

Israel of old, with a minimal amount of written Scripture, had to rely on the prophet for instruction. When he was ignored and dismissed from the public square, knowledge of God decreased until it virtually disappeared.

In the early 1960s, the United States Supreme Court ruled that God was no longer welcome in the public schools of the land. Most of the teachers of that time are either long retired or no longer alive. Their influence is gone. The current classroom teachers are victims of the same lack of knowledge of God's Word. Two or three generations have gone through the school systems never once hearing anything so basic as the Ten Commandments. There are gun-carrying police guarding the halls, and metal detectors at the entrances to ensure weapons are not brought into the school, but since that day, the most basic declaration of God's law has not been heard within the walls of America's public schools.

Again, in the text above we read: ". . . seeing thou hast forgotten the law of thy God, I will also forget thy children." Hardly a day goes by without news stories of young children committing crimes that defy the imagination, and of parents treating their own children worse than a stray dog. We are paying a very high price as a nation because we have "forgotten the law of thy God."

When Ephraim chose his idols, God said, in effect, "Okay, if that is what you prefer, that is what you will get. Don't complain when the chickens come home to roost!"

Chapter 8, verse 7, is the formula: "For they have sown the wind, and they shall reap the whirlwind. . . ." A banker uses a formula to compute interest on a loan. This is a similar concept, in that sowing and reaping are linked. You reap what you sow, and you will reap more than you sow. Sowing to the flesh brings back a crop that in no way reflects God's desires in one's life.

Verse 14 of the same chapter is chilling: "For Israel has forgotten his maker, and buildeth temples; and Judah hath multiplied fenced cities: but I will send a fire upon his cities, and it shall devour the palaces thereof." We have seen fire. We have seen floods. We have seen destruction. We will see even more because God is not about to change His mind about what is right and wrong.

In chapter 10, verses 12–13, is a formula for hope: "Sow to yourselves in righteousness, reap in mercy; break up your fallow ground: for it is time to seek the LORD, till he come and rain righteousness upon you. Ye have plowed wickedness, ye have reaped iniquity; ye have eaten the fruit of lies: because thou didst trust in thy way, in the multitude of thy mighty men."

But verse 14 seems to indicate that, as was the case in Israel, nothing will change: "Therefore shall a tumult arise among thy people, and all thy fortresses shall be spoiled. . . ."

May it not be true that God has said, as He said to Israel of old, "America is joined to idols. Let her alone."

Amos 3:3

Can two walk together,
except they be agreed?

Looking back to verse 2 for context, we find God is telling Israel, "You only have I known of all the families of the earth: therefore I will punish you for all your iniquities. Can two walk together, except they be agreed?"

There was a good relationship between Israel and her God; then there was an increasing apostasy. Little by little, things changed. It was not a sudden turning around, but a subtle whittling away at foundations, devotion, relationship. God's lament is, "You, Israel, are my only love. What happened? I have no choice but to punish you. We no longer have anything in common. I need to get your attention to bring you back to me."

The world encroaches on our love for God. It is too easy to get attached to friends, toys, jobs, or anything else at arm's reach at the expense of our personal relationship with the Lord. We still call ourselves believers, we still go to church, we still read our Bibles and pray, but it is all perfunctory, superficial. We have lost our first love.

We no longer have anything in common, so the relationship is empty. It is not severed, since we cannot lose our salvation. God is not one to break His promises. Eternal is still eternal. But life is empty. No joy. No expectation of what God will do next to bless us.

God hasn't changed since He is the same yesterday, today, and forever. We have changed. Other things have taken His place.

How can two walk together when they have little or nothing in common?

*Then said the Lord,
Doest thou well to be angry?*

Mercy! A prophet with a message and an attitude.

Jonah clearly did not want the job the Lord gave him. *Nineveh—are you serious? Let them stew in their own juices. They deserve what is coming to them. And more!*

Nineveh was one of the most cruel of nations in ancient history. Their brutal handling of others whom they had conquered was legendary. Jonah wanted them to get every drop of God's judgment! Who knows, maybe someone in Jonah's family had been the victim of Nineveh's oppression. All we know is that Jonah did a one-eighty and made a beeline in the opposite direction.

Jonah paid a high price for his disobedience. Rather than make an outright confession of his sin to the Lord, he was willing to be thrown into the sea where he surely would drown. He spent three days of unbelievable behavior modification in the belly of a great fish God had prepared just for him. Later, when back on dry ground, he found a new level of importance for his message and trotted off to Nineveh, shouting to the housetops, "You have forty days to repent or God will destroy you for your wickedness."

What a shock! From the most lowly citizen to the ruler of this important city-state, there was repentance! The people were willing to hear and accept Jonah's message, and to repent. Who would have thought it possible? For well over one hundred years Nineveh was a different country.

One of the lessons learned from this account is that one can never tell how another will respond when hearing the salvation message of the gospel. There are more stories that could be told of God's grace than we will ever hear. For example, one scoundrel spat upon the Bible and refused to listen to anyone who, in love, tried to reach him with the message of God's salvation. Then one day, out of the blue, the tears started to flow, and repentance came to a hardened heart as God moved on his life.

There is hope for a friend, relative, neighbor, husband, or wife for whom you may have prayed for years, having seen no change. James 5:16 encourages us: "The effectual fervent prayer of a righteous man availeth much." Don't give up.

Oh, yes, about Jonah's attitude: Message delivered. Jonah has done his job. Now in your imagination, up on that hill over there, do you see Jonah? He is under that leafy plant in the shade. What do you think he is doing there? He's pouting, wishing God had sent judgment on Nineveh. This is where he had expected to have a ringside seat for the fireworks.

Jonah should be rejoicing in the success of his ministry. Thousands of people have repented and turned to God. Scripture indicates there were at least 120,000 small children, so young that they didn't even know their right hand from their left. Instead of praising God that as many as a million or more people were spared, he wanted a human barbecue!

The book of Jonah ends with this question from the Lord: "And should not I spare Nineveh, that great city, wherein are more than six-score thousand persons that cannot discern between their right hand and their left hand; and also much cattle?"

We don't know Jonah's answer to the question. We can only hope he got his heart right with God. Few evangelists have had such incredible results from their crusades. It would be a shame if Jonah never got to rejoice in the blessing.

All we know of Jonah other than in the book bearing his name is a brief reference to him in 2 Kings 14:25. It seems that God in His mercy still had at least one more job for him to do.

Thus saith the Lord of hosts; Consider your ways

Take a look at yourself. Do an inventory of your thoughts, your motives, your actions, your relationships. See what will happen if you continue in the direction you are going. Is this what you really want for your life? Is this the legacy you want to leave behind?

Here was the situation: The people of Israel lived comfortably in fine homes. The temple, the visible symbol of God's presence among them, was far from complete. Here was the question before the residents of Jerusalem: Do you think it is right for you to live in such comfort when the house of God is little more than a memory?

Twice Haggai challenged Israel to "Consider your ways!" They were paying a high price for forgetting God. Their crops failed, their drink didn't quench their thirst, their clothes were not sufficient to keep them warm, and no matter how much they earned, they couldn't pay their bills. God was judging His people for putting Him at the bottom of their priorities.

Friend, the challenge to consider is ours as well. In a society that is so firmly focused on having things, seeing something in an advertisement and wanting it, keeping up with the Joneses and everyone else on the block, have we forgotten what we owe God?

Paul asked the people of Corinth, "For who maketh thee to differ from another? and what hast thou that thou didst not receive? now if thou didst receive it, why dost thou glory, as if thou hadst not received it?" (1 Corinthians 4:7) The problem has been with humanity from time immemorial. The problem in its rawest form is greed.

Many people think a dollar in the plate when it is passed is enough. Truth be told, a dollar in today's economy doesn't pay for the electricity one person would need while in church, let alone the heat, air conditioning, building upkeep, and salaries. Oh, and what about the missionaries, tracts, lawn mowing, and . . . ? Well, the list could be rather lengthy.

If all we have was received of God, how much do we owe Him? In the Old Testament, one-tenth was required—ten percent. But there was ten percent of wages, of crops, of livestock, of any increase. The total came closer to thirty percent!

It has often been said that we can't outgive God. It is true. While the car will eventually need to be replaced, the roof may need to be fixed or the heater updated, our clothes will wear out and other bills keep going up, God will bless our faithfulness.

When we give with an attitude of gladness for the privilege, God will bless us. In 2 Corinthians 9:6–8 we find a classic passage on giving: "But this I say, He which soweth sparingly shall reap also sparingly; and he which soweth bountifully shall reap also bountifully. Every man according as he purposeth in his heart, so let him give; not grudgingly, or of necessity: for God loveth a cheerful giver. And God is able to make all grace abound toward you; that ye, always having all sufficiency in all things, may abound to every good work. . . ."

The concept here is not to give for the sake of getting more, but to gladly give back to the Lord some of what He has given us. You cannot outgive God. He will never be a debtor to anyone.

Read Haggai 1:4–8.

Is it time for you, O ye, to dwell in your cieled houses, and this house lie waste? Now therefore thus saith the LORD of hosts; Consider your ways. Ye have sown much, and bring in little; ye eat, but ye have not enough; ye drink, but ye are not filled with drink; ye clothe you, but there is none warm; and he that earneth wages earneth wages to put it into a bag with holes. Thus saith the LORD of hosts; Consider your

ways. Go up to the mountain, and bring wood, and build the house;
and I will take pleasure in it, and I will be glorified, saith the LORD.

We have our homes, cars, vacations, cable TV, pension plans, and full refrigerators. What have we given God?

Some say, "I can't afford to give anything to God. I can hardly meet my obligations now." Consider your ways! God should be at the top of the list on our budget. Bring what is due to Him and He will take pleasure in it and be glorified. He might also patch the holes in your bag, allow your crops to yield more, and stretch your budget farther than you expect.

One hundred percent without God's blessing is much less than 90, 80, or even 70 percent with God's blessing.

Something to think about!

Conclusion

There are no more "One Liners" on our list, but there are two other short verses that deserve mention before we close the back cover.

Consider Revelation 22:20, which contains the last quotation in Scripture from the Lord: "Surely I come quickly. Amen." If that was the whole verse, it would have been a "One Liner."

Many Bible teachers point to Daniel 12:4 as an indicator of God's prophetic time clock: "But thou, O Daniel, shut up the words, and seal the book, even to the time of the end: many shall run to and fro, and knowledge shall be increased." We are living in a world that is a far cry from what the disciples knew at the time of Christ. Modern technology, science, transportation, and communication are just a few of the advances we enjoy in our lives every day.

Surely, we are living in an historic time that points to the return of the Savior. We believe we are living in the end time. Reference is made by Christ in the Olivet Discourse to the increase of earthquakes and other major disturbances that will affect large portions of the globe. Today we are seeing a dramatic increase in the frequency and severity of weather events, a fact easily confirmed in an up-to-date world almanac. Hardly a day goes by that the United States does not experience a major event with far-reaching consequences on the economy and peoples' lives.

It does not take someone with an advanced college degree to see that something is going on here on planet Earth that does not speak well to our long-term future.

> Fear, and the pit, and the snare, are upon thee, O inhabitant of the
> earth. And it shall come to pass, that he who fleeth from the noise of

the fear shall fall into the pit; and he that cometh up out of the midst of the pit shall be taken in the snare: for the windows from on high are open, and the foundations of the earth do shake. The earth is utterly broken down, the earth is clean dissolved, the earth is moved exceedingly. The earth shall reel to and fro like a drunkard, and shall be removed like a cottage; and the transgression thereof shall be heavy upon it; and it shall fall, and not rise again. And it shall come to pass in that day, that the LORD shall punish the host of the high ones that are on high, and the kings of the earth upon the earth.

—Isaiah 24:17–21

Additional verses in this passage could be cited as well.

It is interesting to note that the kings who have ruled the earth are slated for judgment. Presidents, kings, dictators, and other rulers are going to be brought to account for their personal and national wickedness. They had the power to issue decrees, and many people rose or fell as the result of their decisions. Most of the dictators of the world in just the last hundred years are well known for their crimes against God and men. Their punishment will be certain at the hands of God.

For that matter, this is true of all who have ever lived on earth. Punishment awaits! Sinless perfection is not attainable in this temporal life, so each of us will need to stand before God's judgment bar for sentencing because we have broken God's law. Our appearance will be either at the Great White Throne judgment, where all who have rejected God's offer of mercy and salvation will be judged, or we will stand before the Throne of Grace, with our sins forgiven and clothed in Christ's righteousness because He took our place and punishment when He was our sacrifice for sin on Calvary.

In 1 John 1:5–10 we read these encouraging words:

This then is the message which we have heard of him, and declare unto you, that God is light, and in him is no darkness at all. If we say that we have fellowship with him, and walk in darkness, we lie, and do not the truth: But if we walk in the light, as he is in the light, we have fellowship one with another, and the blood of Jesus Christ his Son cleanseth us from all sin. If we say that we have no sin, we deceive ourselves, and the truth is not in us. If we confess our sins, he is faithful and just to forgive us our sins, and to cleanse us from all unrighteousness. If we say that we have not sinned, we make him a liar, and his word is not in us.

Jesus took our punishment when He hung on the cross. He will forgive us of our sins if we just ask Him to do so. If pride gets in the way, if we try to blow off our sin as though it is not a big thing, saying "a loving God would never send someone to Hell," we make Him a liar. Before you turn the last page of this book, please be sure you are sure. Be sure you are not depending on a baptismal certificate, church membership, or something your parents said you did years back but for which you have no recollection. Do not even rely on a prayer you may have made at an altar during a revival meeting. Many people will walk an aisle at a moment of conviction or parrot back a prayer someone gives them, but a few moments later when they get up to go about their business, there is no change in their life.

One key to knowing you are saved is how you have lived your life after you made a profession of faith. There should be a difference you can see, and that your family and friends can see, too. If there is not a change, and if you have no desire for reading your Bible, prayer, and fellowship with other believers, you would do well to take inventory.

In John 10:10–11, Jesus referred to Satan as a thief when He said: "The thief cometh not, but for to steal, and to kill, and to destroy: I am come that they might have life, and that they might have it more abundantly. I am the good shepherd: the good shepherd giveth his life for the sheep." How Satan would love to make people secure in their false belief that because they joined a church, got baptized, gave money, prayed a prayer, or did some act of penance, they are saved.

Titus 3:5–7 clearly teaches that we can't earn or buy salvation. "Not by works of righteousness which we have done, but according to his mercy he saved us, by the washing of regeneration, and renewing of the Holy Ghost; Which he shed on us abundantly through Jesus Christ our Saviour; That being justified by his grace, we should be made heirs according to the hope of eternal life."

If you are not sure you have ever asked Jesus to be your Savior, if you have doubts about your salvation, or know you have never trusted in what Christ did on the cross, in the quietness of your heart ask Him to forgive you now. He will. Luke 19:10 promises that ". . . the Son of man is come to seek and to save that which was lost." In John 6:37, Jesus adds, ". . . him that cometh to me I will in no wise cast out."

When He died, He was buried, but three days later, He did what was humanly impossible: He arose from the dead to prove He had paid our debt for sin. All of the other "great religious leaders" of the world have a tomb, grave, or other location pointed to as their final resting place. They are dead as a door nail. Jesus Christ is alive forevermore!

Hebrews 7:25 is the promise you can grasp securely: "Wherefore he is able also to save them to the uttermost that come unto God by him, seeing he ever liveth to make intercession for them."

It doesn't matter what you have done. God will forgive. His Son, Jesus, is the defense attorney for you before the high court of Heaven. The guilty verdict that by rights you must plead has been vacated by the One Who paid your penalty with His own precious blood.

This same Jesus Who walked on earth two thousand years ago is coming back again. We believe it will be soon. Everything points to sooner rather than later. If you have trusted Jesus as your Savior, you will spend eternity with Him, and you can anxiously pray the last prayer in the Bible in Revelation 22:20, which we will quote as our last "One Liner:" ***"Even so, come, Lord Jesus."***

Afterword

We called them "God's One Liners," but what we found in these shortest verses in the Word of God is that they are long on meaning and importance. Foundation stones are usually the larger ones upon which smaller ones rest, but in these examples are found some bedrock truths upon which we can build our lives, our faith, and our eternal future.

It is our prayer that these simple thoughts have encouraged you to be more diligent about the study of the Word, and that as a result, all of us will take an extra moment to pay heed to even the little details.